Douglas A. Puryear

Helping People
in Crisis

Jossey-Bass Publishers
San Francisco • Washington • London • 1979

HELPING PEOPLE IN CRISIS
A Practical, Family-Oriented Approach to Effective Crisis Intervention
by Douglas A. Puryear

Copyright © 1979 by: Jossey-Bass, Inc., Publishers
433 California Street
San Francisco, California 94104

&

Jossey-Bass Limited
28 Banner Street
London EC1Y 8QE

Library of Congress Cataloging in Publication Data

Puryear, Douglas A   1938–
    Helping people in crisis.

    (The Jossey-Bass social and behavioral science
series)
    Bibliography: p.
    Includes index.
    1. Crisis intervention (Psychiatry)
2. Family psychotherapy.   I. Title.
RC480.6.P87   616.8′915   79-88108
ISBN 0-87589-421-6

Manufactured in the United States of America

JACKET DESIGN BY WILLI BAUM

FIRST EDITION

Code 7924

The Jossey-Bass
Social and Behavioral Science Series

Preface

This book is written for all
those who work at helping people and who thereby get
involved with people who are having crises. The coverage is
directed to a wide range of practitioners, including both
people who deal specifically with crisis intervention and people who encounter crisis situations as an incidental development in their work. Much of the material has been presented
in seminars or workshops attended by physicians, juvenile
probation counselors, social workers, psychiatrists, psycholo-
gists, ministers, nurses, and other counselors—a wide range
indeed. The book is meant to be most practical, presenting a
system of crisis intervention and spelling out in detail "how to
do it." It is basic enough to provide an adequate foundation
and procedural guidelines for the beginner in this work, but

its strength lies in its organized system, which will be useful to the beginning and the experienced counselor alike.

Crisis intervention is a specific method for helping people who are in crisis resolve their crises successfully, in a safe and healthy way. Characteristic of this approach is intensive work over a short time that emphasizes the current situation and facilitating the client's capacity to help himself. Crisis intervention is stressful but very rewarding; one can see concrete results in a short time.

Crisis intervention is gaining increasing recognition in the mental health field. It is an area where several newer trends in mental health converge—including working with families, short-term therapies, and the use of paraprofessionals. Its approach is based on a specific theoretical foundation, and it is applicable to specific types of problems.

Although the system presented in *Helping People in Crisis* stresses a family approach, it is equally applicable to work with individuals. It is a methodical, thoughtful system, so that the worker can deal with a crisis in an organized fashion. One advantage is that it minimizes use of the worker's time while effectively benefiting the client.

I am indebted to those workers who have taken my crisis intervention course, thereby teaching me more about the subject and providing some of the case examples; to the patients, who have taught me most; to the other workers and writers whose ideas I have liberally borrowed; and to my family, who have persistently asked, "Are you *still* working on that book?"

Towson, Maryland   Douglas A. Puryear
August 1979

Contents

ix

x

The Author

DOUGLAS A. PURYEAR is a
clinical supervisor at the Sheppard and Enoch Pratt Hospital
(Towson, Md.) and a psychiatrist in private practice. He is also
the court psychiatrist for the Circuit Court of Baltimore
County, where he specializes in juveniles and their families,
and serves as a consultant to the Maryland Departments
of Social Services and Juvenile Services.

Puryear was born in McAllen, Texas, in 1938. He was
awarded the B.A. degree in physics (1960) from Rice University and the M.D. degree (1964) from the University of Texas
Southwestern Medical School. He interned in medicine and
pediatrics at the University of Arkansas Medical Center and
completed his psychiatric residency at Sheppard Pratt in 1968.
Puryear has been a staff member of the Aiken County Mental

Health Center (Aiken, S.C.), the University of Georgia Medical School, and the Sinai Hospital Psychiatric Clinic (Baltimore, Md.). Currently, he is presenting courses in family work and in crisis intervention for the Departments of Social Services and Juvenile Services in Baltimore and Carroll Counties and at the Sheppard Pratt School of Mental Health. In addition, he is conducting research studies of youths who appear before the Juvenile Court and of their families.

Helping People in Crisis

A Practical, Family-Oriented Approach to Effective Crisis Intervention

Chapter One

People in Crisis: An Introduction

You may be a probation officer, a psychologist, a social worker, a general practitioner, a counselor, or a psychiatrist. You find yourself in your office facing Father, Mother, and fifteen-year-old Judy. Father is angry, stating emphatically that no matter what you say, he will not allow his daughter to date a seventeen-year-old junkie. Judy quietly says she *will* date Don. Father slams his fist on the chair and storms, "That's it! I'm through. You're not living in my house any more, starting now!"

What do you do now? Better yet, is there any way to prevent the situation from reaching this crisis point? *Helping People in Crisis* will help answer these questions. This book presents an organized system that emphasizes understanding, thinking, and planning, so that a crisis situation can be dealt with in a logical, organized, and systematic way. The result of this approach is efficiency, which minimizes the time demanded of the worker while maximizing the concrete benefits to the clients.

A fundamental premise is that there are a basic foundation of knowledge that can be learned and specific skills that can be acquired. With these, a crisis situation can be approached in an organized, systematic way. At any given moment workers can know what they're doing, why they're doing it, and what they'll probably need to do next. This knowledge will increase both workers' confidence and their effectiveness; happily, these two factors further reinforce each other.

Crisis intervention is an approach to helping people in crisis. Characteristically this approach consists of intensive work over a short period of time, with emphasis on the concrete facts of the current situation and on the client's own efforts at changing it. The crisis intervention work is aimed at resolving the crisis in a healthy and successful way.

Crisis intervention is not psychotherapy in my view, although it is related to some types of family therapy. In comparison to family or individual therapy, crisis intervention has a narrower and more superficial focus, more modest goals, and briefer duration. I practice both individual and family therapy, and I am not in any way demeaning their value. In fact, some families in crisis may begin family therapy immediately, while others may eventually be referred for therapy. For most families in crisis, however, crisis intervention is the treatment of choice, and efforts at therapy or at referral for therapy will merely lead to misunderstanding, frustration, and a lost case.

For the purpose of clarity and ease of learning, I will focus on crisis as a strictly defined and very limited concept in this book. Once the material is grasped, it can be flexibly applied. Much of it will be useful outside this narrowly defined range, and some of it will have wider application than just crisis intervention.

The basic ideas of crisis intervention presented here derived from work with individuals. Most of these ideas will apply equally well to families, and I believe that working with a family is usually the best way to approach crisis intervention. Most of the statements in this book can be applied either to families or to individual clients, so they should be read with that understanding.

The goal of the approach presented here is effectiveness in helping a family or a client and at the same time efficiency in the use of that scarce commodity, time. Specifically, this approach is designed to achieve an effective crisis resolution by using from one to six sessions, ranging from thirty to ninety minutes, plus a few phone calls. The complete involvement for each case should require from one up to a maximum of eight hours of the worker's time. At that point the crisis should be resolved, and hopefully the family will be functioning in a somewhat healthier way than before the crisis. This approach can also be used in dealing with crises that arise in the course of long-term involvement with a case; the previous relationship would be resumed once the crisis was resolved.

The theoretical basis underlying this approach is derived from systems theory, personality theory, and crisis theory. Such theories are not necessarily true in any absolute sense but are useful to the extent that they help us to think about and predict human interaction and to plan interventions logically. We think of the family and the individual in terms of systems and subsystems, with various forces and relationships balancing each other and with any change triggering counteracting changes, so that a state of equilibrium results.

Although humans have a drive to grow, any tendency to change is threatening to the security of the system. For example, in some families, the father remains distant, while the mother fills her needs by close involvement with a child. If the child begins to become more independent, the mother may withdraw some of her attention and support. Without adequate support the child is not able to sustain his or her move toward independence and the status quo is maintained.

The various human systems generally fluctuate narrowly around their baseline state of equilibrium. There tends to be little change over short periods of time; change occurs only slowly over longer periods. A crisis situation can result when the balancing process begins to fail and equilibrium is disrupted. Any factor that tends to shift the equilibrium state, especially if it does so rapidly and especially if in a displeasing or undesired direction, constitutes a *problem*. Any problem that is not quickly, easily, and almost automatically countered (resolved) constitutes a *stress*. This produces notable discomfort (anxiety and tension) and will prompt attempts to solve the problem and thus return the system to the status quo (equilibrium).

An individual's sense of security can be viewed as depending on his relationships with others, whereby he obtains four basic emotional needs—*relatedness* to others, *support* from others, a sense of *self* with separateness and an identity, and *self-esteem*, which is derived largely through input from others.

At equilibrium, our relationships with others exist in a state of dynamic balance. Much of our behavior is determined by our need to maintain our relationships so as to safeguard security. We might wish to improve relationships, yet we fear that changes may turn out for the worse. Any tendency toward change threatens our security, and any loss or threatened loss of security can produce uncomfortable anxiety, tension, or depression. This stimulates us to act to restore equilibrium. Crisis can result when change cannot be quickly counteracted. Then change tends to lead to further changes and a state of disequilibrium, with more discomfort and a sense of turmoil. If there are inadequacies in our perception of what's happening, in our support network, or in our repertoire of coping mechanisms, our efforts to control the process will be hampered, disequilibrium will persist, and a crisis state may develop.

In crisis intervention work, mere involvement will provide the clients with some support and relatedness, while maintaining an appropriate professional attitude, without excessive closeness or intrusiveness, will help to maintain the client's sense of self. Thus, much of the worker's action in crisis intervention will be aimed at raising the client's self-esteem. In therapy, with the support of a long-term relationship and with a goal of personality change, a therapist can confront his patients and risk threatening their self-esteem. In crisis intervention, this is to be avoided. By raising the client's self-esteem, a therapist simultaneously decreases his defensiveness, helps reverse the crisis process, activates him, and quickly builds rapport.

We all deal with many problems and many threats or potential threats to our security every day. Often we deal with them so easily and quickly that we hardly notice them. To do so we have each developed our particular set of *coping mechanisms,* those ways in which we typically resolve problems, maintain equilibrium, and thus protect and maintain our security.

The internal coping mechanisms—the psychological defenses of rationalization, denial, suppression, and so on—are a subclass of coping mechanisms. In crisis intervention we are generally more interested in the external and concrete ways of responding to problems—the external coping mechanisms. For example, when faced with a difficult problem, I may go to the library for a book on the subject or I may consult a friend. Of course, families also have their typical sets of coping mechanisms. If my family has a problem, my wife being mildly ill for example, we might hold a family conference to determine adjustments, or we might ask Grandma to come stay a while. Other family coping mechanisms might be to pray, throw a party, or pick on one family member. Some other individual coping mechanisms might be to beat my wife, take a vacation, or get drunk.

The usual coping mechanisms are not always adequate for resolving a given problem for various reasons: (1) A problem may be just too great or too overwhelming—the death of a family member, for example. (2) A problem may have some special personal significance that makes it overwhelming. One man may adjust relatively easily to the loss of a limb, while the same loss may represent overwhelming stress to another man, perhaps because of his occupation or because of some more interpersonal symbolic meaning. (3) A problem might occur at a time of special vulnerability—I might ordinarily handle a flooded basement with relative equanimity, but if it occurs while I'm recovering from the flu, it might seem like a catastrophe. A series of problems within a short time may deplete a person's ability to cope. (4) A problem may come when a person's usual coping mechanisms are blocked—my wife may have just left me, and so I can't discuss a new problem with her as I usually do. (5) A problem may occur for which a person is unprepared because it is new to him and he has never developed applicable coping mechanisms. For example, if I handle all my family problems by taking charge and giving orders, the blossoming adolescence of my first child may eventually leave me feeling helpless.

For a variety of reasons, then, a person or a family may not be able to resolve a problem with their usual coping mechanisms. This produces a great deal of tension and discomfort, people focus their attention on the problem, they mobilize their efforts, and their *secondary coping mechanisms* are brought into play. This simply means that previously unused or rarely used coping mechanisms are tried. These moves may be more extreme than those that the family usually uses, or they may be simple enough but just not in the family's usual repertoire. These secondary mechanisms may resolve the problem. If so, the experience usually represents an episode of growth for the family members. They have survived a stress and developed a new skill, and they will probably be in a better position to deal with the next threatening problem. If, however, their secondary coping mechanisms also fail to resolve the problem, they will enter a state of crisis (see Figure 1).

The definition of a *crisis* is a special state during an ongoing process of disequilibrium in a person or a group. The state results when both usual and secondary coping mechanisms fail to resolve a problem. The state of crisis is characterized by:

1. Symptoms of stress, primarily psychological and physiological (depression, headache, anxiety, bleeding ulcer). There is always extreme discomfort.
2. Attitude of panic or defeat. A person who has tried every way he can to solve a problem and has failed feels overwhelmed, inadequate, and helpless. He will tend to be either *agitated*, with unproductive behavior aimed at discharging tension (fast driving, beating up someone, pacing,

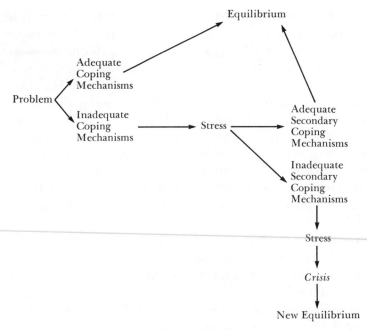

Figure 1.   The Crisis Process.

drinking), or he will tend to be *apathetic* (retreating into bed or into a drunken stupor).

3. Focus on relief. In this state a person is primarily interested in relief of the pain of stress—the headache, the depression—and the initial problem may even be half forgotten. There is little gathering or noticing of new facts or new ideas, and little organized effort at problem solving. Relief will generally be sought by discharge behavior, withdrawal behavior, or turning to others for rescue.

4. Lowered efficiency. In this state a person may continue to function normally, but his efficiency is markedly lowered, and those problem-solving efforts that persist are inefficient.

5. Limited duration. People cannot exist in this state for long—it is unbearable. It will end and a state of equilibrium be regained within a maximum of six weeks. This is supported by clinical experience and by some research.

The state of equilibrium attained after a crisis may be at a level of functioning that is the same as, higher than, or lower than before. For example, a man whose problem involved his job may decide that he is disabled and take on a new role, achieving a new equilibrium as a nonworker. However, a worker may learn a new skill after becoming disabled and actually attain a better position. If a crisis has been resolved successfully, the person or family may be much stronger. They may have grown individually or as a family. They may have opened up lines of communication and developed new coping skills. They may see that they are stronger than they thought. Their self-image may be improved, and they may be less likely to go into a crisis when a new problem arises. In another case, the resolution itself may contain the seeds for the next crisis.

The following story will illustrate a number of these points. While serving involuntarily in the army, I was required to provide nighttime psychiatric coverage for the emergency room. I had to be available by telephone and come in to the hospital whenever necessary.

One night my sleep was interrupted at about 2:00 A.M. by the telephone. "Dr. Puryear? Dr. Smith would like you to come to the emergency room." It was the emergency room nurse.

"What's the problem?"

"Dr. Smith would like you to come in now."

This was strange, since the emergency room doctor himself would usually call the covering doctor to discuss the case, and together they would decide if the covering doctor should come in. The situation was also slightly touchy, since I did not want to come in on an unnecessary trip. In the final analysis, however, Dr. Smith probably had the authority to order me to come in. I became more subtle. "What's the problem?"

"Dr. Smith wants you to come in now."

"Well, could I speak with Dr. Smith?"

"No."

"Why not?"

"He's with the patient right now."

"Well, what's wrong with the patient?"

This was the crucial question apparently, for now the awful truth was revealed in the nurse's hoarsest stage whisper, "He's got a gun!"

At that point it was not too difficult to restrain any impulse I might have felt to leap from my bed, throw on my clothes, and race to the emergency room at 2:00 A.M. in order to practice my psychiatric skills on a patient with a gun. Rather, clinging fast to my warm bed several miles and a few thick walls away from the emergency room—and from the man with his gun—I asked if I could speak to the patient. I seemed to make some progress; she gave him the phone.

"What do you want?" he asked.

"What do *you* want?" I countered.

"I want to be admitted to the psychiatric ward."

Possibly only those who have been in the army within the past fifteen years will recognize what a plum gaining admission to a psychiatric ward can be—how greatly to be desired. Although in the army I had little power and small authority, I did have the authority to admit people to the psychiatric ward. "Well, then, give the doctor your gun and I'll have him admit you to the psychiatric ward."

"OK."

The doctor confirmed that he now had possession of the gun; I directed him to write the order admitting the patient. I then hung up the phone, pulled the covers more tightly around me, and, as best I can recall, went back to sleep.

To consider some points: Was this a crisis? If so, for whom?

I think this may have been a crisis; if so, it was a very acute one—especially for the doctor. He probably had symptoms of stress, some sense of panic, a wish for relief, and lowered efficiency. The nurse may also have been in a state of crisis. Was the patient in a state of crisis? I think not. I think he had found a secondary coping mechanism and was using it very effectively. Was I in a state of crisis? Certainly not, because I had more sense than to go to the emergency room where, upon being confronted by a man with a gun, I presumably would have soon been in a state of crisis myself.

To clarify some concepts: There were four people—the

doctor, the nurse, the patient, and me—involved in a difficult situation. Some of us may have been in a state of crisis, and some of us not. If anyone involved was in a state of crisis, we could call this a crisis situation. The patient had a problem, and his resultant behavior was certainly causing a problem for the rest of us and thus may have caused a crisis. But, though someone's behavior or someone's symptoms may *cause* a crisis or reflect the existence of his or her own crisis, a behavior or a symptom cannot be said to *be* a crisis. Similarly, though a problem may cause a crisis, a problem, even a serious problem, cannot be said to *be* a crisis. People sometimes consider the idea of an emergency as being identical with a crisis. An emergency can be defined as any state requiring immediate action to prevent dire consequences, usually threat to life or limb. Thus, if the patient was about to shoot someone, the emergency room situation was an emergency. If any one of the four of us was in a state of crisis, the situation was a crisis. So an emergency may or may not also be a crisis, and a crisis may or may not also be an emergency. The two terms are not identical. Finally, a crisis is *not* any situation where someone calls and says "This is an emergency" or "I'm in a crisis."

One of the first rules of mental health work is to survive. You can do very little to help your clients if you are dead or psychiatrically disabled yourself. Second, it is useful to recognize your own capabilities and limitations. For example, I do not specialize in people with guns. Third, it is important not to let your client's crisis become a crisis for you, or else you won't be very effective. Finally, the main point illustrated by this story is the importance of not accepting others' definitions of a situation, not letting them define it for you, whether it's someone saying "You must come" or "This is an emergency" or "This is a crisis." Gather the data and make the decision and the definition yourself. Presumably you are in a better position to be objective than those more closely involved—as clearly illustrated by the army story.

To repeat, a crisis is a state in which people have failed to resolve a problem, are in disequilibrium, and exhibit the first four of the five characteristics of a crisis—symptoms of stress, attitude of panic or defeat, focus upon relief, and decreased efficiency. The fifth characteristic, limited duration, will not be determined for a particular crisis until the crisis is over. However, if the particular state (showing the first four factors) has lasted without significant change for over six weeks, it is probably not a crisis but a state of equilibrium. Thus a person or group of people is in a crisis if the defined characteristics are exhibited, and a situation is referred to as a crisis if someone or some group in the situation is in a state of crisis. On occasion we may refer to a group of people, such as a family or the staff in an emergency room, as being in a crisis if the definition applies to the group as a whole, even though it does not necessarily apply to any one group member. I do not use the term *crisis* to refer to any situation in which there is turmoil, pressure, anxiety, or a sense of urgency. I hold to the specific definition.

According to the definition, the peculiar—though by no means rare—condition of constantly being in a state of "crisis" is also not a crisis, but a state of equilibrium. Consider a family in which the father gets drunk every weekend and beats his wife, who is sleeping with the milkman, while the children are frequently truant and use drugs. This situation is not a crisis but this family's equilibrium. The family may need help; they may even want help, but crisis intervention is not called for. Now, if some *change* occurs, if the father loses his job or is arrested for assault, then the family may or may not develop a crisis, depending on their ability to cope with the new problem. (If they do develop a crisis, crisis intervention will be warranted and can help them return at least to their previous level of equilibrium.)

A useful way of understanding crisis theory and of assessing a particular crisis situation is provided in Aquilera and Messick's book on crisis intervention.* In this approach one specifies the state of equilibrium of the family and the problem that has initiated the crisis process. The theory is that

*D. C. Aquilera and J. M. Messick, *Crisis Intervention: Theory and Methodology* (St. Louis: Mosby, 1974).

a problem will not lead to a crisis unless there are deficiencies in one or more balancing factors. These balancing factors are (1) adequate perception, (2) adequate network, and (3) adequate coping mechanisms. In the discussion up to this point, adequate perception and network have been subsumed under coping mechanism; henceforth, they will be addressed as distinct entities.

By *perception* we mean the way the problem is viewed or defined by the family, the meaning it carries for them. For example, when it is discovered that fourteen-year-old Bonnie is pregnant, she is perceived as "ruined," and the underlying perception is that the parents have been "failures." Perception is generally adequate to the extent that it is factual and realistic.

By *network* we mean the social supportive network, the group of other people and agencies with which the family has social contact and who give support during a crisis. This might include grandparents, friends, teachers, or a church. The network is adequate to the extent that there are enough contacts and that they are supportive and helpful in the face of the particular problem. This adequacy would be in contrast to the grandmother who drives twenty-five miles to scream hysterically that Bonnie is "ruined, ruined, ruined" and that she is a slut just like her mother, and then collapses with chest pains that the family must attend to (unless, of course, this temporary diversion is seen as useful).

Coping mechanisms are adequate to the extent that a family's usual repertoire of mechanisms are applicable to the particular problem situation. For example, I may always go out and get drunk when the kids present problems, thus leaving the field clear for my wife to handle things. This effective coping mechanism will not be applicable if one of my children becomes seriously injured while my wife is out of state visiting her mother or while she is seriously ill.

In applying the model shown in Figure 2, we state the unresolved problem and describe the equilibrium state. We list each balancing factor and fill in any inadequacies that interfered with resolving the problem before a crisis developed. We particularly ask why this problem led to a crisis at this time,

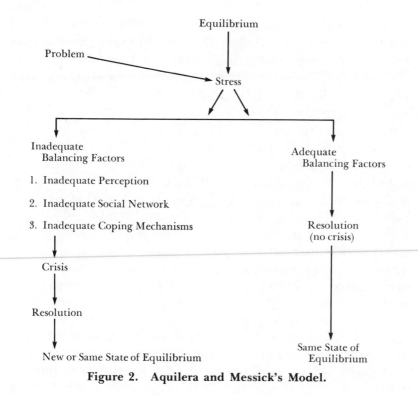

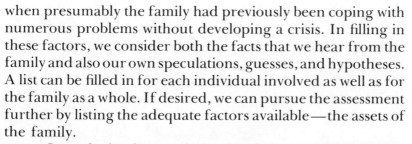

Figure 2. Aquilera and Messick's Model.

when presumably the family had previously been coping with numerous problems without developing a crisis. In filling in these factors, we consider both the facts that we hear from the family and also our own speculations, guesses, and hypotheses. A list can be filled in for each individual involved as well as for the family as a whole. If desired, we can pursue the assessment further by listing the adequate factors available—the assets of the family.

Once the inadequate balancing factors are listed, some approaches toward resolving the crisis will become self-evident. The problem then will be to devise strategies leading to the development of the needed balancing factors. For reasons that will become clear later, in practice I usually define the unresolved problem—the Problem—after filling in the lists rather than before.

A partially analyzed example will clarify this system.

Consider the Jones family, consisting of Mother, Father, and Junior. Father works hard and keeps to himself. Mother is the backbone of the family, handling most problems competently and getting support from her close-knit family of origin when needed. Junior is a bright eleven-year-old, somewhat overly close to his mother. (This describes the Joneses' equilibrium.) Father gets a promotion and the family moves from Louisiana to Pennsylvania. Shortly thereafter, Mother fractures her leg on the ice and begins a long hospitalization, involving two operations. Father hires a parttime housekeeper. Things go well at first, but after a while Father starts drinking a bit. He then has several conferences at school because of Junior's falling grades and mild misbehavior. Mother starts getting depressed and criticizes Father and his handling of things. Father develops insomnia and loses all patience with Junior, and he starts to berate Junior constantly. Junior runs away. Father, drunk, drives around looking for Junior and is arrested for running a stop sign. He nearly assaults the officer, catches himself, becomes very frightened, and on the officer's advice calls a crisis clinic. From an interview we learn the above and (partially) fill in Aquilera and Messick's lists as follows: Equilibrium: Father works hard, keeps to himself; Mother handles any problems, gets support from family of origin; Junior overly close to Mother.

Problem: Mother's illness (more specifically, the family's difficulty adjusting to Mother's illness)
Inadequate perceptions:
> *Father:*   1. "If I'm a man, I should be able to run things without help."
> 2. "My eleven-year-old son should behave maturely and responsibly."
> *Mother:*   1. "My husband is seriously damaging my son."
> 2. "My son can't survive without me."

Inadequate network:
> *Family:*   1. in new town, without friends, cut off from Mother's family

        2. unaware of social work services in hospital
           and community
Inadequate coping mechanisms:
    Father: 1. no experience in dealing with Junior and
                   his problems
                2. Mother unavailable to rely on
    Junior: no experience functioning without Mother
    Mother: energy depleted by illness

This example illustrates how a crisis develops when the usual balancing factors are inadequate for dealing with a particular problem, how the symptoms of the crisis (Father's traffic violation, for example) are quite different from the problem that led to the crisis, and how this type of approach to assessment already suggests some strategies for intervention. It also illustrates the use of the worker's guesses to make hypotheses, rather than relying solely on the data.

During a crisis, the original problem is unresolved. Furthermore, it may well have gotten lost in the shuffle. People made efforts to cope, there were reactions to those efforts, and then reactions to those reactions. One person's efforts at tension discharge may have produced the stress that precipitated a crisis in another person. A given situation may represent a crisis for one person, for several persons, or for a whole family. Obviously the picture can rapidly get quite complicated. In working with the crisis, we must try to distinguish the unresolved initial problem from the coping efforts, the symptoms of stress, and the efforts at relief, as well as trying to clarify who is in crisis.

As an exercise, we will sort these factors out of the following example of a crisis situation, which was related by a crisis intervention student:

Mrs. T took her two girls and left her husband a year ago after learning of his sexual involvement with Lisa, their teenaged daughter. Her own involvement with Lisa was rather stormy, and she worried that the experience with the father might lead Lisa into promiscuity. Mr. T committed suicide some five months after the separation. Mrs. T recently began dating, and soon after a neighbor complained about Mrs. T's noisy late-night comings and goings and the girls' noisiness. Mrs. T feared she might be evicted. She had difficulty with a fellow employee, began to complain of nerves, and gave two weeks' notice at work. There was no other job in sight. Shortly thereafter she came home at 1:30 A.M. and found her daughter and a number of teenage friends in the apartment with some beer. In the ensuing argument she struck Lisa on the back and leg with a shoe, bruising her. Lisa ran away and also reported her mother on a charge of child abuse.

This led to Mrs. T's referral to social services. At that point she seemed unable to function. She was not cooking meals or housecleaning, and she did not seem to be supervising her younger daughter. She complained of stomach pain and was not eating, although her doctor found no medical problem. She insisted that her hitting her daughter was of no significance and blamed all difficulties on her late husband and the bad influence of Lisa's friends.

The worker was able to get Lisa and her mother to meet together with a professional and found temporary living arrangements for Lisa to provide a cooling off period. The mother's functioning improved, her stomach pain stopped, and her appetite returned. Lisa returned to live with her mother and sister, probably returning to much the same stormy type of equilibrium as before.

Trying to sort this situation out can easily lead to confusion. This is a complex and unclear situation, and important data are lacking. I think the case clearly meets the definition of crisis for Mrs. T. There may have been some earlier crises, but this one seems to have been precipitated by Mr. T's suicide, to which the family was unable to adjust. The noisy partying may represent use of an inadequate coping mechanism. The mother's hitting Lisa was a discharge of tension; the stomach pains were symptoms of stress. We hear nothing of an external supportive network, and the family members don't seem to have been able to support each other. Although we don't know how the family perceived the suicide, we can assume the mother's perception of the problem was not adequate for problem solving.

Now, it is quite possible to sort all this out differently. We might say the threatened eviction, the job problem, or the daughter's unruliness or running away was the precipitating problem. We might say Lisa or the whole family was in crisis. We particularly need more data about the family's functioning prior to these various events. Though our definition of crisis is clear, in real life things frequently aren't clear-cut. This is a difficulty, but as will become clear later, one that can be turned to advantage.

The need to clarify just who is in crisis may arise frequently, perhaps in dealing with parents or even with other professionals. Most workers are familiar with calls from frantic parents who say that their children are "having a terrible problem" or, in one way or another, are in a crisis. It often turns out, of course, that the child is in no crisis at all—he or she appears to be quite happily using drugs, flunking out of school, or being promiscuous. Clearly the crisis is the parents', not the child's. A crisis intervention procedure—including the child whenever possible, but focusing on the distress of the family as a whole or of the parents alone—may be a useful approach. Occasionally all that can be done is to help the parents to perceive the situation accurately in terms of everyone's limitations and limited ability to change things, and the parents can be helped to cope with that reality. Sometimes the child's behavior then improves notably without direct intervention aimed at his or her behavior. Sometimes it doesn't.

Sometimes a situation represents a crisis, not for anyone in the family, but for a worker or agency involved with the family. An example of this was a request by a worker for urgent help for a thirteen-year-old boy who had been placed in the training school—a very bleak situation. The worker was quite concerned about the boy, who he described as constantly crying. Some questioning and a telephone call revealed that the boy was actually functioning reasonably well in the training school. However, when the worker, who had selected the boy for counseling, saw him on weekly visits and began discussing the boy's home and family, the boy inevitably began sobbing. The worker was quite uncomfortable with this, at least partly because it unleashed upon him the full impact of what the boy was going through in this situation. None of the worker's words of cheer, comfort, advice, or coercion could stop the boy's flow of tears. Since, however, the boy was functioning adequately, I would guess that these opportunities to let loose some very appropriate tears were helpful to the boy. The crisis here, if one existed, was not the boy's but the worker's, and it arose partly because of the worker's misconception of what was happening and his use of inappropriate mechanisms to cope with his own discomfort, that is, trying to stop the crying. Some clarification of these points coupled with some support seemed to resolve the worker's crisis.

I have defined crisis rather strictly, and in these terms most workers would not see a true crisis very often. In actual practice, a worker frequently becomes involved in the process before the state of actual crisis is reached. The pain and turmoil of the precrisis disequilibrium may be sufficient to prompt a request for help from the family, or the worker may become involved through some other means—for example, as a part of a legal process. In these precrisis situations, the theory, principles, and the process are the same as in a crisis, and the worker tries to help the family avert the impending crisis, while hopefully still helping the family to grow. Frequently, the worker also becomes involved after the crisis is over and a new equilibrium is already established. This crisis intervention approach may still be of some use, especially if the worker tries to review the crisis with the family, but it is much more difficult for the approach to be effective then. Often the worker can merely establish some contact, and if the new equilibrium is a poor one, he or she can try to be available if another crisis occurs.

Crisis is a time of openness to intervention, a time of marked decrease in the defensiveness with which people protect their security and resist change. It is a time when a resistant family may become involved with a worker and be willing to implement some of the worker's recommendations. In fact, a few family therapists advocate deliberately provoking crises within the course of therapy in order to make the system open to change. Of course, they stress the need to provide careful guidance and support to keep the crisis under control. Thus, a crisis may be a time of opportunity.

This chapter has presented the basic theory of crisis. The term has been defined, a crisis has been described, and a few general principles have been discussed. In following chapters, the basic principles of crisis intervention will be given, followed by the seven steps of intervention, with applicable techniques interspersed at the relevant points. In use, the principles serve as guidelines, the steps as an orderly plan, and the techniques as specialized tools. It will become clear how all of the material merges into an internally consistent, interlocking, organized approach. The principles logically evolve from the theory, and each principle tends to promote some of the other principles. This fitting together continues through the discussion of the steps and techniques.

For example, it is clear that crisis leads to turmoil and to lowered self-esteem, which leads to passivity, and it is clear how turmoil and passivity lead to yet lower self-esteem. Our principle of problem solving creates order, which decreases the turmoil. Problem solving also diminishes the passivity, thereby enhancing self-esteem. It also conveys hope and expectations, which raises self-esteem. Further, focusing on problem solving serves as an avenue by which the worker takes charge—an important part of the worker's first step.

Chapter Two

Principles of Crisis Intervention

There are eight basic principles to follow in crisis intervention. These principles spell out areas of concern and effective attitudes for approaching these areas. The principles should underlie all of the work and activities in crisis intervention and should remain constantly in the back of the worker's mind. The eight principles are: (1) immediate intervention, (2) action, (3) limited goal, (4) hope and expectations, (5) support, (6) focused problem solving, (7) self-image, and (8) self-reliance.

I want to give an overview of each of these principles and show how everything fits together. Then I will go into each principle in some detail.

1. Immediate intervention. A crisis is a time of danger, and a time-limited opportunity for intervention. When someone asks for help, you try to decide if there is a crisis. If there is, you should see them right away.
2. Action. In crisis intervention, the worker very actively

participates in and directs the process of assessing the situation and, together with the client, of formulating a plan of action for the client to pursue.

3. Limited goal. The minimal goal of crisis intervention is to avert catastrophe. The basic overall goal is to restore the client to his equilibrium state, hopefully with some growth also occurring.

4. Hope and expectations. The worker must initially instill hope into the situation. He does this through his whole approach, including his attitude and his expectations of the client and about the situation.

5. Support. The worker must provide a great deal of support to the client, primarily by being "with him," available to go through the process with him. The support must be carefully given so that it is sufficient without being excessive.

6. Focused problem solving. This is the backbone of crisis intervention; it provides the structure that shapes and supports the whole process. Basically, we try to determine The Problem—the basic unresolved problem that led to the crisis—and then assist the client in planning and putting into action steps aimed at resolving it. We keep our own and the client's attention focused on that problem and on the problem-solving process, and we avoid being distracted and sidetracked.

7. Self-image. Efforts must be made to assess and understand the client's self-image, to consider carefully the effect that any of the intervention maneuvers might have upon it, and to protect and enhance it. These efforts will pay off in many ways, including increased rapport, decreased defensiveness, and mobilization of the client's energies.

8. Self-reliance. From the very onset, attention must be paid to fostering self-reliance and combating dependency. This need must be carefully balanced with the need for support.

Immediate Intervention

People in a crisis are in a state of turmoil and great distress and may be in actual danger. At the same time, they are in a state of great opportunity if the crisis is handled properly. These two points, the danger and the opportunity, plus the time-limited nature of the situation, dictate the need for immediate intervention; that is, you need to respond at the time they ask. Putting people on a waiting list is one way to screen for "good" therapy cases—they are the ones who will still keep an appointment after a two-week wait—but the waiting list has no place in crisis intervention.

People cannot long tolerate the stress of a crisis. They will resolve it in some way, usually within a maximum of six weeks from the time that they enter the crisis state. Some state of equilibrium will be attained. This end state and the way of reaching it may be favorable or unfavorable. The family may wind up stronger, with new skills and improved relationships, and they may reach a better state of equilibrium than before. However, the nature of the crisis state—including the tension, the sense of urgency, the misperceptions, and the decreased efficiency—means that many attempts will be made for quick resolution or for quick tension relief, attempts that will not be well thought out and that may be inappropriate and counter-productive. Some of the problem-solving efforts and tension discharge maneuvers that people use during the crisis may result in harm to themselves or others, may worsen the overall situation, or may plant the seeds for further difficulties.

At worst, the crisis may be ended by disaster—suicide, homicide, or chronic psychosis. A fourth type of disastrous ending is permanent disintegration of the family unit. All forms of leaving the family unit are not necessarily disasters by any means, but cutting off a family member—severing com-munication and acknowledged emotional ties, with a resultant loss of belonging and of identity as being a part of the family—usually is. I say severing of *acknowledged* emotional ties because the ties remain, unresolved, unacknowledged, and unavailable for resolving, and they cause problems. Such a cut-off can cause serious, chronic problems for both the excluded member and for the rest of the family. Thus I include a cutoff as one of the four possible disasters that may result from a crisis. The first goal of crisis intervention may be merely to avert a disastrous outcome, and we should not forget in our therapeutic zeal that achieving that goal may be no small accomplishment.

Another danger we meet in the crisis situation is that of missed opportunity. I have spoken of the strength and rigidity of the homeostatic process with which equilibrium is maintained and change resisted. I have also spoken of the human drive for growth. Although growth can occur quietly and slowly, we find that frequently growth and crisis appear simultaneously. This fact reflects the stress involved in adjusting to the changes of growth. It also reflects the fact that the unsettled turmoil of crisis actually presents a state of relative flexibility during which growth may occur. Crisis is a time when people are most accessible and least defensive. The relatively rigid homeostatic processes and the reinforcing equilibrium relationships are disrupted. People have unsuccessfully tried their routine approaches and are open to trying new ones. They may precipitously resolve the crisis in some way, but in the meantime they frequently are unusually receptive to forming a working relationship with a helping person. This is an opportunity, and the crisis state is time limited. This means that if you're ever going to have a positive impact on this family, *now* is the time.

I've discussed the dangers of a crisis situation—the danger of a disastrous ending, the chance of someone's actions making things worse, the possibility of an unhealthy adaptive process leading to a less stable or less functional level of equilibrium, and the danger of the missed opportunity. For all these reasons, when you are approached by people who are truly in crisis, you need to see them immediately. By immediately, I mean sometime between this moment and tomorrow night, that is, with no more than one night passing before a meeting. If it is impossible to see the people immediately, then a brief chat or telephone conversation is essential to establish some rapport and to provide some support until a full meeting can be arranged.

During any first contact preliminary to an appointment, you should obtain a few basic facts, but in the case of crisis intervention you must go a bit further. You can ask a few

stions to help you assess the true urgency of the situation
l to get some idea of whether it represents a crisis. You will
...ed to determine who is to come to the first meeting—
usually the more people the better. You might even suggest
some task for the client, such as obtaining some particular
information or document to bring to the interview. You may
on occasion arrange for the client to call you again before the
interview or for you to call the client for some purpose. This
arrangement depends on the time lag before the appointment
and your estimation of the urgency and the need for support.

At the same time, you must also carefully limit the
conversation. You do not want to get too involved or the client
will expect you to provide magical solutions, that is, "answers,"
over the telephone, and things will get off to a negative start as
the client becomes disappointed by your failure to do so. You
also do not want to hear too much of the story at this point, or
the client will be less primed to talk when you do meet. This
also might make it more difficult for you to direct the flow of
discussion in the first meeting—you'll already know too much
and repetition will seem foolish. Also, other family members
may see you as the caller's ally against them or otherwise feel at
a disadvantage.

Thus, control the conversation, get what you need, and
get out. This first brief chat will establish some tie between you
and the client, who will know that you are a real person, are
available, and are involved with him. This fact alone will
provide some support and relief from tension. However,
remember that this first contact is only a necessary preliminary
step and a small stop gap before the crucial first full meeting.
Ideally, no more than one night should pass before that
meeting. If the meeting can't be arranged within a few days,
the client should be referred to some other resource where
help can be obtained immediately. If that is also impossible,
you can try to maintain the client by telephone contacts until
he can be seen. This can be a difficult and ticklish task. If you
reach this point very often with people who are in crisis, you
might need to examine the workings of your particular system, your own perception of the workings of your system, and

the way you and your system define *crisis*. Something needs to change, because the first principle of crisis intervention is *immediate intervention*.

Action

Patients for psychotherapy can be placed on a waiting list (although I don't advise it), but people in a crisis need to be seen immediately, and things have to start happening right away. The prototype for traditional psychotherapy is a therapist who primarily listens, making occasional comments where indicated. The primary focus in therapy is on understanding, especially of the patient's inner processes and of their reflection in his behavior and interactions with others. The therapist's activities are designed to facilitate the patient's expressing and observing of his internal workings, so that the patient's understanding increases. With increased understanding the patient has more self-awareness, more self-control, and more options, options that now can be selected on the basis of a well-informed, contemplative decision-making process rather than of neurotic factors of which the patient is but dimly aware. The achievement of this state represents a fairly long-term goal, achieved with a good bit of work, frustration, experience, and time. Psychotherapy by and large focuses on this process of understanding, and the patient is left to apply his understanding when and as he chooses, although of course the application may well be subject to scrutiny also. All of this is as it should be—but not for crisis intervention.

Crisis intervention is an active technique, and the focus is on action. People in a crisis tend to be immobilized, doing nothing, or to flounder about, discharging tension. People in the precrisis state of the crisis process are utilizing secondary coping mechanisms, hoping that they are effectively directing their efforts toward resolution of the problem in a constructive fashion. Sometimes they are, but sometimes they are floundering their way into a crisis. Whether immobilized, discharging tension, or floundering in precrisis, these crisis clients need to start moving in a purposeful, coordinated,

-directed fashion. They need to feel that something is
g done, both for them and by them, and they need to feel
this right from the first session.

Inactive and indirect processes—such as filling out
questionnaires, lengthy and leisurely explorations of issues or
feelings or history, getting to know each other today and
coming back next week—won't work for crisis intervention.
The worker must be active. You actively participate in, con-
tribute to, and direct the session. You listen enough so that the
client feels listened to and understood, but most of your
listening occurs in the course of actively gathering information. The information gathering is in the service of understanding the problem (not so much understanding the person)
and formulating a clear statement of the problem so that there
can be active work toward the goal of resolving it. This
understanding and formulation of the problem are done
together with the client, as a team. Then, together with the
client, you begin to develop a plan for dealing with the
problem, and this plan involves some specific concrete actions,
preferably action by the client. Then, with the plan formulated, you actively assist, encourage, and push the client to
initiate the action.

Now, ideally this action will be some appropriate and
direct step toward resolving the problem. That is not always
immediately possible, however. Perhaps the client's resistances
or other reality factors block a direct step, perhaps the client
can't accept or acknowledge the nature of the problem, or
perhaps the worker and client have just not been able to figure
out the problem yet. Nevertheless, it is essential that the client
leave the first session in the process of doing something. Even
doing something that won't directly help with the problem
itself is much better than doing nothing. So, we see to it that
the clients leave the first session with a task to do.

We might note that processes like ventilating feelings,
clarifying viewpoints, and fostering communication among
family members could be considered "doing something."
These things are indeed important and will be used at times
during the sessions, but they usually just aren't enough for the

crisis client. The "doing something," the action, needs to be something more concrete. Thus, in contrast to psychotherapy, the crisis intervention process has short-term goals of resolving the problem and the crisis within a few weeks, the worker is quite active, and the emphasis of the session is ultimately on action.

Limited Goal

The goal of crisis intervention is to restore equilibrium, ideally at the same or a better level of functioning than before the crisis and with some degree of growth. The minimal goal is to avert catastrophe—suicide, homicide, chronic psychosis, or family disintegration. The goal is *not* personality change or change in the family structure, that is, change in the basic pattern of functioning. This is extremely important to understand.

If our first family from Chapter One—Father drunk and beating Mother every weekend, Mother sleeping with milkman, kids truant and using drugs—should enter a crisis (say, due to Father losing his job, the kid's arrest, or Mother's pregnancy), the basic goal of crisis intervention would be to restore equilibrium, that is, father being drunk and beating Mother every weekend, and so on.

A suicide or other catastrophe may have been averted, and the family may have even grown stronger. Seeds may have been planted for future change. Family communications may be slightly improved, people's self-image and perception of other family members may be slightly changed, and the family's social network may have been expanded. Some of these slight changes may have a ripple effect and lead to other changes. Something that was said or done may lie dormant, fermenting in a family member's mind for a while, only to produce change in the future. At the least, the family will have hopefully established contact with a worker or agency that they perceive as a helpful resource. The family may be more receptive to help in the future if the worker or agency responded to the crisis as the family wished and did not interfere

with other areas of their life or try to push someone into
something, like therapy or Alcoholics Anonymous.

If you pick inappropriate goals—for example, trying to
stop the father's drinking—this may worsen the crisis or its
outcome and will almost certainly render the help ineffective,
frustrate both you and the family, and decrease the chance
that the family will ever ask for help in the future.

To follow the preceding example further, this family
has functioned in a state of equilibrium with Father's drinking
for years. If one of the boys is arrested for possession of
marijuana, this may lead to a crisis state for any of a variety of
reasons—paying an attorney's fee, threatening Father's job
due to his taking time off for court, or causing Grandmother
to berate Mother as being to blame for the boy's behavior. Any
of these factors may lead to other incidents in the crisis
process, such as Father assaulting the cop who arrested the
boy, or whatever.

Now, we know that Father's drinking may have something to do with the *dynamics* of the boy's being arrested for
possession of pot. However, his drinking really has very little
to do with the development of the *crisis* at this time. This is
true even though the family may present themselves with
Mother berates Father for drinking or even with Father
berates himself. If you begin to focus on Father's drinking,
you will merely be allying yourself with Mother, who has
bitched about it for years (although claiming inability to *do*
anything about it). This will immediately make you the enemy
of Father; all of his alcoholic, magical, passive-resistive defenses will come into play, and your ability to be effective in the
situation will be quite diminished. Your job is to help the
family return to equilibrium, possibly with some growth.
There is a paradox here; that is, if you can focus on the
problem-solving return to equilibrium as the goal and carefully follow the principles, some growth will probably occur. If
you make an effort to foster growth, however, you will probably fail, and you will also fail in your crisis intervention.

Now, I anticipate an argument, and I half agree with it.
This crisis, with its turmoil, stress, and reaching for help, may
be just the time to finally *do something* about Father's drinking.

Principles of Crisis Intervention

Maybe you can get him to start A.A. Maybe *now* you can ̩ the family into family therapy. I'm doing the family a disse vice by neglecting the drinking and by helping them resolve the crisis. That may be right. One of the world's best family therapists may be able to do all that and provide tremendous growth and benefit to this family. Unfortunately, in my experience, it might take one of the world's best family therapists. I only know four or five people of such calibre, and I ain't one of them, and the others are probably too busy to take the case. In the meantime, I'll try to restore equilibrium without catastrophe, hope a little growth occurs or that one of the seeds I drop might sprout later.

For example, when Mother complains bitterly about Father's drinking, I might say, "I see you're really concerned about this; maybe you'd get something out of some Alanon meetings." Then I'd listen to forty-nine reasons why she can't attend, and twelve reasons why it wouldn't help, and three reasons why she went or a friend told her about it or she almost went and it didn't do any good and really didn't fit her situation. I'd reply, "Oh," and then go on with the focused problem solving about the crisis. Now I've planted a seed in Mother's head, and I've indicated that if this concerns her maybe *she* should do something about it, and I've told Father that I think he's an alcoholic without him feeling obligated to argue with me about it. Who knows, these seeds might sprout.

I don't want to overstate the case. If the father should suddenly begin to beg me to tell him how to contact A.A., or if the parents should plead with me to refer them for family therapy, I would try to persuade them that they really didn't want to get into that, but if they persisted, I'd probably give in.

I'll discuss these ideas about paradox, referral, and alcoholism later on. Meanwhile, I'll settle for return to equilibrium, no catastrophes, and a few seeds.

Hope and Expectations

Except for the one great hope that someone else can magically cure their problems, people in crisis feel hopeless.

One of your primary jobs is to instill hope. This is accomplished largely by your attitude.

As the worker, you promise nothing, but you expect a great deal. From the beginning you are using the active problem-solving approach, which lends itself beautifully to this concept. You quickly engage yourself and the client in assessing the problem and making plans for those actions that will lead to its resolution. The process itself clearly states your expectations. You expect the crisis to be resolved in some way (you know it will be), you expect problems to be worked out, and you expect your clients to function, to work with you. Generally all of this is not spelled out verbally but is clearly illustrated by your whole approach. These expectations on your part generate hope in the clients, improve their self-esteem, change their self-image, and help to activate them.

Clearly, this approach is different from giving reassurance, which can be deadly. "Don't worry, I know everything will be all right." To the client, such reassurance implies either that you're lying, since you can't know the future, or that you haven't listened to him, because he feels things are hopeless. Reassurance, in fact, can usually be translated: "Listening to your problems and feelings makes me feel bad and uncomfortable; I don't know what to do either, I feel just as helpless as you do, and I wish you'd just stop talking to me about it."

Also, reassurance can lead to tangential discussions or even arguments with the client, which are a waste of time: "I'm sure this will work out." "Yeah, but, . . ." and you're into it. The time is better spent on planning *how* the client can work it out or on actively trying to work it out in the session if appropriate.

Consider this exchange:

"I know you'll be able to find a job."

"Yeah, but didn't I just finish showing you my wooden leg?"

Compare that exchange with this one:

"Sounds like getting a job is really hard. What do you see as the first area to try?"

"Well, somewhere that doesn't mind the wooden leg."

Principles of Crisis Intervention

The problem-focused approach is actually a *positive* approach than the reassurance.

It is sometimes useful to ask about past crises and how they were resolved. This is of some help in assessing the current problem, as you'll want to know why the same approaches didn't work this time, but it is used largely as another means of instilling hope. When things get so terrible, a person begins to feel that they've always been terrible. A reminder of these past crises (by just asking about them) helps the client to see himself as a person who has handled things before. Again, this is more effective if it is not spelled out to the client ("See, you can handle problems even when things look bad."). This is better dealt with indirectly, either by just going over the story and then ending it ("So that settled the situation?") or somewhat more directly ("So even after all that you were able to work yourself out of the jam?"). As the client reviews these past crises that he has survived, his self-image changes and his hope is rekindled.

Support

We have earlier noted that the lack of an adequate social network, of adequate support from other people, is one of the factors that determines if a particular problem develops into a crisis. A major aspect of intervening in a crisis is providing support. This support must initially be provided by the worker. A large degree of this support is usually provided by telephone, by just being available, on call. During the time of crisis, clients will tend to call for a variety of apparent reasons. Usually the fundamental reason for the call is to gain and maintain your support and the feelings of security and relief that go with it. Frequently the calls will be "urgent." Calls from the client must be returned, promptly if possible. However, it is generally preferable not to return a call immediately. Knowledge that you will call gives some support, and with a delay of perhaps thirty minutes, the person may calm down, do some thinking, and begin to handle his own feelings or immediate problem. Frequently the "emergency" will have been resolved by the time you call. This reduces the tendency

for the client to see you as the magical problem-solver or the
handler of all upset feelings (which lowers their self-reliance
and ultimately lowers their feelings of self-esteem). Yet you
must return calls soon enough that the patient perceives you
as a reliable means of support. Of course, some calls are
returned sooner than others, for example, if you feel a person
has a significant risk of suicide. You will need to give most
crisis clients (if truly in active crisis) your home telephone
number. If you have other resources available, such as an
agency, clinic, or treatment team, you can give their numbers.
This reduces your load. Nonetheless, you must provide,
personally or otherwise, a continuous reliable source of support, especially at the beginning.

Once the support is established, there are a number of
ways to reduce the pressure of this load on you and at the
same time to protect the client's self-esteem. I usually give the
client my office and home numbers, and frequently (depending on my assessment of the situation) I emphasize that they
can call at any time. I also explain any obstacles that they
might find in trying to reach me. Frequently, just doing these
things gives enough support and reassurance that the client
does not need to call. If you haven't offered, the client feels
less secure. He may struggle with himself about calling and
then finally call. Whether or not you feel annoyed, the client
will feel he is intruding on you and will feel in a begging
position. This further lowers his self-esteem and sense of
security with you. He may then require several extra phone
calls to test you out. In this work you will get some 2 A.M.
phone calls. They should be handled with as much grace and
understanding as you can muster at that time. Some clients
will make several of these calls until they are assured that you
are available and receptive, and then they will stop calling. A
rare client will begin to abuse this, and then limits will have to
be set with kindness, but quite firmly. There are many ways to
set these limits, such as allowing no calls except during working hours, giving a "hot line" number, allowing one night call
a week only, setting a time limit on the conversation, and so
on. These restrictions are applied in terms of your assessment
of the client's real needs.

The best way to handle inconvenient calls is to anticipate the problem. You can tell the client you will call him to check on some information or on the result of some task tomorrow at 2 P.M.—in other words, fit his emergency calls into your schedule. You might also, depending on the situation, just call to "see how you're doing." However, this tends to suggest helplessness or excessive dependency on the client's part, and it might convey an undesired message of lowered expectations, thus lowering the client's self-esteem.

Obviously, I use the telephone as a major instrument in the whole process of crisis intervention. I would feel rather lost without it. In circumstances where phones are not available, the work is much more difficult and requires a great deal of ingenuity. You can consider *any* available phones—at the grocery store, barber shop, or pool hall. Perhaps you can set up something of a communications network with a police radio or the local patrolman's walkie-talkie. There can be verbal contacts or notes passed through school or church. This will sometimes require a great deal of resourcefulness.

As a basic principle, you should try to enlarge and strengthen the client's social network as soon as possible. This will not only reduce the demands on you but will also provide resources that will help resolve the crisis and reduce the potential for crisis in the future. In building a network, you frequently must first try to diminish hostility between immediate family members so that they can receive some support from each other. This is often ineffective or insufficient. Next you want to enlarge the network. This is done first by inquiring about relatives. I never ask who is available to help; instead I find out who exists. This saves having to struggle through hearing that there is "no one." Ask such questions as: "Where are you from?" "Your family still lives there?" "Are you still in touch?" "Any relative near here?" Other resources are ministers, agencies, friends, neighbors, school counselors, and anyone else you can imagine.

These resources are used in a variety of ways. Grandmother may come in twice a week and cook. The minister may introduce parents to other parents who are also struggling with raising an adolescent. Neighbors may provide transportation on a short-term basis. Some babysitting may enable Mother to get a part-time job. A friend may tutor Junior. These resources are useful for the concrete services they provide. These services may merely decrease some of the pressures of daily life on the clients while they struggle with their crisis. Frequently these services may play a more direct role in the plan of attack on the problem underlying the crisis. Further, totally aside from the concrete services provided, receiving support from others is of fundamental value in struggling with a crisis. Finally, this whole process widens the social network, strengthening the family and establishing useful relationships for the future.

    The workers's role will likely include some degree of supporting the supporters. They may find themselves undergoing significant emotional stress in maintaining their supportive role. Also you do not want Grandma called in to help and have her advising, "Don't worry, just don't think about it." This would undermine your approach to the crisis. A situation in which the helpers are not only not helpful but actually harmful can be ticklish. You can try to encourage any helpful aspects of their efforts. A good principle is to enlist the helpers for specific tasks. Then they feel less confused and inadequate, feel more useful, and are less likely to function in misguided and nonhelpful ways. If Grandmother can be asked to make soup, she may not need to give so much advice, and this small assistance to the family may be quite helpful.

    A major principle in providing support is to provide as much as is necessary (and at the very first, perhaps even some extra as a margin of safety) but in general to diminish your support as soon as feasible, providing no more support than is necessary. You do not want to foster excessive or prolonged dependency on yourself, to promote unrealistic expectations of you, or to overload yourself.

Focused Problem Solving

    Problem solving is the backbone of the crisis intervention approach. There may be some overlying difficulties that must be worked through first—animosity due to tension discharge efforts, for example (the husband just beat up the wife and she resents it). But as soon as possible, efforts should be focused on the job of solving the underlying unresolved problem—The Problem—which initiated the crisis process.

In our theory of crisis, this Problem must be resolved in some fashion in order to regain equilibrium. In practicing crisis intervention, we go somewhat further and claim that the resolution of this problem resolves the crisis. We may believe that this is literally true, or we may simply hold that this is merely a useful idea.

Holding the view that resolving The Problem is the way to resolve the crisis is valuable. It provides us with an organizing principle for our work with the client. It also provides us with something to do, in an organized way, that makes sense to the client while support, ventilation, activities, shifted focus, improved relationships, and time lead to a crisis resolution without catastrophe. So, we hold this concept either because we believe it or because it is useful—it works. I maintain that it doesn't matter what we believe about this concept but that it is important to proceed as though we believe firmly and quite literally that resolving The Problem resolves the crisis.

In this way we are led into a problem-solving approach to crisis intervention. But this careful focus on problem solving serves other purposes also. It serves to define and clarify for the client both the nature of the intervention process and the role of the worker. It diminishes the personal animosities and blaming processes that may have arisen in the family, and it interrupts preoccupation with personal symptoms and grievances. Everyone shifts attention to the more impersonal Problem. This focus provides a track for the crisis intervention process to follow and provides a channel for mobilizing energies into concrete goal-directed action, so that the client can begin to feel he's accomplishing something. Your attitude and approach ("Let's figure out what the problem is and see how we can try to solve it") provides a leverage for changing the client's perception of himself and of the situation—to move him away from "Who's to blame for this hopeless mess?", for example. Thus, the approach itself begins to alter the crisis state.

In the later discussion of assessment it will become clear that how you define The Problem to be worked on is crucial. Here I will merely point out that there are usually many possible ways to define The Problem, and it is essential to choose a definition that lends itself to the problem-solving process. You need a problem that is "workable," that is, something that can be changed. For example, you would never define The Problem as "Mother died" but as "the family hasn't yet adjusted to Mother's death."

The problem-solving focus helps define your role as worker. You are not an expert in living who knows how other people should live and who can easily see what others should do to resolve their problems. Most of the clients will not be stupid. If their problems had easy, simple solutions that they could apply, they would have solved them without seeking help. If you are dealing with a crisis state and can see an easy, simple solution, watch out! You have misunderstood something, missed something, or have not been provided with some critical information. There are rare exceptions to this, such as when the client is just unaware of some important fact—for example, what does and does not cause pregnancy or what particular service is available in the community. If you find that such lack of knowledge appears to be the case, by all means provide the information, but it is still advisable to proceed with caution—chances are high that you have missed something.

So, you are not an expert at solving clients' problems for them. You are an expert in the process of problem solving— that is, how to go about doing it—and you have skills at assisting people as they go about working out their problems. This is another of those things that you will probably not spell out verbally but will communicate more loudly, clearly, and effectively by your attitude and approach.

At the beginning, try to focus on defining The Problem and then try to keep the focus on solving it. This means avoiding tangents, such as what John did to Mary fifteen years ago. Obviously you focus this way only as much as the client can tolerate. You might just have to hear about what John did to Mary, but as soon as possible, relate the story to the current problem and get back to it ("Oh, I see, because that happened fifteen years ago, then Tuesday when he said he was leaving, you thought he meant forever, or you wondered if he had a girl friend, so no wonder you were so upset on Wednesday.").

Feelings are a special issue. They don't fit neatly into the problem-solving framework, but they must be attended to. In certain traumatic situations, such as soon after a death in the family or the birth of a malformed or stillborn child, assisting with feelings may be a major part of the intervention. The intervention may occur shortly after such an event. At such a time, a brief period of crisis may even be part of the normal grief reaction. If this period is not properly handled by a person, the person may develop a crisis state later. The feelings will have to be dealt with then.

In an early intervention, shortly after the event, one principle is to help the client face reality but in manageable doses, not too much at one time. Knowledge is a major tool, generally preferable to ignorance and fantasies. Therefore, things must be faced, and the facts should be discussed. For a gross example, it is probably better for the mother to see the dead baby once and perhaps even to hold it. It is better to let someone know the facts about a serious illness, their own or someone else's. These facts can be given over a period of time, according to the interest or withdrawal shown by the person. The facts can be presented with a slight vagueness, so that the person can choose to not quite hear them if he wants or to ask for more details if he wishes. Eventually, the facts must be faced.*

Therefore, it is important to provide a supportive situation in which a person can be helped and encouraged to go through the painful, upsetting, and necessary work of grieving. The person can be provided temporary relief from

---

*See G. Caplan, *Principles of Preventive Psychiatry* (New York: Basic Books, 1964), for further discussion of this topic.

some of the pressures of daily living, both to offer support and to facilitate the grieving. The person may also need some temporary relief from the grieving. He may go to bed for a time, but he then should be encouraged to arise and deal with the situation some more. The relief should generally be partial and intermittent—in "doses"—with the person also encouraged to get on with the grieving work. The person needs understanding acceptance of his feelings, and here ventilation is encouraged. This means gently helping the person to talk about the situation and express his feelings—again, perhaps not all at once, but in manageable doses. Active listening can be of great use here.

One of the things that needs to be supported and accepted is the person's being "upset." Unfortunately, people are upset by seeing other people upset, and the normal tendency is to try to make them stop being upset—by medication, empty reassurance, exhortation, criticism, and so on. However, for healthy adjustment to a traumatic event or loss, the feelings need to be experienced and expressed. The bereaved widow who "handles it beautifully" is a prime candidate for a serious depression later on. The feelings have to be dealt with and the grief work done sooner or later.

Such a traumatic situation may present a crisis or a semicrisis, either in an acute state at the time of the event or later when a delayed reaction erupts. The supportive approach just described can help a person handle the situation and the resulting feelings healthily with appropriate grieving. Crisis intervention may be needed in cases where this was not done, where people are dealing with a delayed or postponed reaction. This frequently presents itself as some form of depression, although it may appear in a disguised form—the delinquent act of a youngster, for example. In these cases, then, The Problem might be defined as "the client has not yet dealt with his feelings about something." This concept does bring feelings into the problem-solving framework. I think that in these somewhat special cases, crisis intervention sometimes comes closest to resembling therapy.

An example is an elderly lady whose husband died. She "handled it beautifully," meaning she only shed a few proper and discreet tears, played the gracious hostess to friends and relatives who gathered for the rituals, and caused no one any distress by displaying grief. She continued to do quite well afterwards, displaying a surprising self-sufficiency, learning to handle unfamiliar chores that her husband had previously managed, and finding various activities that afforded her satisfaction. She did quite well, in fact, until she and the family decided she should move across town to an apartment that would be less expensive and nearer some of her relatives. She began to have trouble making decisions about the details of this move. Then she began having trouble sleeping, lost her appetite, and became fretful. In short, she began exhibiting signs of depression.

She was eventually seen in consultation, primarily regarding her inability to make the decisions necessary to carry out the move. The Problem was defined as "You have not yet dealt with your feelings about your husband's death, so you're not ready to give up some of the belongings that still hold your attachment to him." We talked about this and about her husband. We set a task for her to make an inventory of her belongings, one room at a time. Her eldest daughter moved in with her for two days to assist with this task, and they completed it. While so engaged, they had many opportunities to discuss Dad and various memories connected with the various belongings. Mrs. M cried a moderate amount on these two days. After the inventory was completed, Mrs. M went across town to take measurements of the rooms of a typical apartment, her next task. We then discussed which articles might or might not fit. While discussing some of the articles she came near to tears but did not cry, although I gently encouraged her to do so. By then her symptoms were abating and she began to make some decisions, although with some difficulty. She did a few more tasks, one of which was to spend a weekend at the house of her relatives "to get the feel of the neighborhood," which offered further opportunities for some

reminiscing about her husband. She made the move and did
quite well in her new location, becoming very active in volunteer work.

In general, feelings are dealt with only as much as
necessary in crisis intervention. Some ventilation or exploration of feelings may be initially encouraged, but it is not often
desirable to be digging for unexpressed feelings. In crisis
intervention, feelings may be regarded by and large as obstacles that must be dealt with before the work of problem
solving can properly proceed. Feelings can usually be dealt
with by the active listening techniques. Once the client has
released some pressure by ventilating some feelings in a
controlled and receptive situation, you can become more
active in establishing the connections between the feelings
expressed and The Problem, for example, how feelings led to
misperception ("Oh, I see, at that point you were so mad that
whatever he said would've sounded like an insult, and that's
when you walked out" or "I understand now, you were feeling
so down that any job seemed like an impossible chore, so then
you just went to bed"). You can attempt to keep the expression
of feelings focused on how the feelings relate to The Problem,
limiting the expression to those feelings that are directly
related or to those that are interfering with the problem
solving. Frequently, for example, people in a family crisis
begin their first session with hostility, blaming and scapegoating each other. Your efforts should be aimed at rapidly
shifting the focus from feelings to problem solving. As just
described, one way to approach this is to just accept each
feeling and then quickly tie it into attempts to understand the
evolution of the crisis. This changes the set from ventilation of
feelings with escalating emotionality to rational exploration.

By *set* I mean the participants' expectation and perception of the ongoing process—what they look for, what they
expect to happen, and the manner in which they anticipate
that they will participate. Clients may enter the interviews with
any of a wide variety of sets, for example, an argumentative set
("We'll continue our battle here."), a judicial set ("We'll each
present our sides and you judge who's right."), or a magical set

("We'll tell you our problem and you'll solve it."). Some people enter with a purely emotional set ("Emoting is good; we'll all vigorously emote."). The client's set forms a part of the atmosphere. The atmosphere, however, is the worker's responsibility, so part of your job is to direct and control the set. As one aspect of this, you want to engage the clients in *thinking* as soon as possible, and the focused problem-solving approach facilitates this. Then, of course, the thinking facilitates the actual work of problem solving.

Self-Image

Each person experiencing crisis, whether personally, through a family crisis, or through the crisis of a family member, will approach the intervention in his own way. The most common ways are in anger, venting it at the worker or at others; in passivity, awaiting help; in desperation, demanding help; or sometimes in a state of cooperative denial, offering to help you help these other poor people who have problems. Whatever the approach, we can assume that people with any of these reactions have something in common—their approach in part reflects their way of dealing with underlying feelings of anxiety and of low self-esteem—a bad self-image. Their self-image problem is probably most frequently revealed through anger, and the process is most clearly illustrated by discussing the person who approaches in anger.

The person coming for help is either in crisis himself or is involved in a crisis. A person in crisis is at the end of his rope, having tried everything he knows and can think of. He has finally succumbed. He has not been able to help himself and has come to you for help. He sees himself as a helpless failure. Similarly, the involved person who is not personally in crisis has struggled through the process of problems, primary and secondary coping efforts, great stress, and various unsuccessful interactions with others. He has not been able to help the others, which damages his self-image as a capable, helping person. This, along with other factors and processes in the turmoil, makes him mad at them, which damages his self-image as a compassionate person. Further, during all this stress, his own tension-relieving efforts may have damaged the others, which further lowers his opinion of himself.

So, whether in crisis or involved in one, a client may try to protect his self-image, to feel more capable and less guilty, by blaming others. *They* caused it, *they* mismanaged it, and *they* are still interfering with his obviously reasonable methods of resolving it. He will manifest anger toward those who have contributed to his worsened self-image or toward anyone who threatens to do so further. In this state he comes to you for help. This may be the last thing in the world he wants to do. He expects you to dig into him and expose his inadequacies and faults and to condemn him. He sees himself as a failure, a bad parent, a worse spouse, a nothing. He fully expects you not only to agree with this assessment but to take great pains to point out the particulars to him and to his family.

Therefore, he may approach you with belligerence and antagonism as one way of clutching and protecting the last shreds of his self-esteem. You can gauge the degree of damage or threat of damage to his self-image by the intensity of his belligerence. He may approach you with his hostility focused elsewhere, perhaps at a family member who is labeled "the problem." You may gauge the intensity of his feeling himself to be a failure as a parent, for example, by the amount of vehemence with which he denounces his child. Of course, not all clients deal with these self-image problems with overt anger. A client may try to appease you and win your support and sympathy with a more congenial approach, but most likely this merely covers some similar negative feelings about himself and some frightened, angry, negative expectations of you and of the intervention.

Your job, then, in the face of all this negative feeling is to make a consistent effort to raise and to protect the client's self-esteem. There are various general and specific measures you can use. Certainly, you will give a certain amount of thought to what you say and how you say it. Further, you can treat the client, his attitudes, and his viewpoints with courtesy and respect. You can show some interest in nonproblem aspects of his life—his hobbies, occupation, past accomplishments, and so on. You can take care regarding the label he will bear in the meetings—is he "the alcoholic" or "the hard worker"? The desired labels can be emphasized by commenting on them and working them into your formulation of the crisis process ("I see, so when you came home half exhausted from working at that blast furnace all day, you walked into this situation."). You should take pains to divert attacks by other family members on a person's self esteem. One method is to focus on the attacker rather than the attacked ("I see, when he drinks like that you get angry, you're scared about what will happen, and that's how you were Tuesday when you were yelling at your son?"). Another method is to change the subject. (These concepts are discussed more fully in Chapter Four).

It is best not to encourage the client to blame others for his problems, as this leads to guilt, estrangement, and further lowering of self-esteem. Suggest only tasks that you think the client will do and that he will surely succeed at, especially in the beginning. You should not do things for the client that he can do for himself. Your attitudes, words, and actions should all be guided by concern for the client's self-esteem.

The client sees himself as an inadequate, helpless failure. You are attempting to convey by your entire approach your attitude that the client is a capable, decent person who has been temporarily overwhelmed by extreme stresses, and who will use your help to cope with these stresses and get back on the track. This implies your appreciation for his level of equilibrium, whatever it may be, as a state in which he is a productive person who is coping with the many problems of everyday life. Based on this attitude, you will have expectations of the client. You will expect him to collaborate with you, to formulate ideas, and to be doing things to promote the problem-solving process. To have these expectations therefore further conveys the attitude. I emphasize here that this attitude and these expectations should be conveyed not by explicitly stating them but by what you *do* during the interview.

As this view of the client becomes obvious to him, and as

your efforts to protect his self-esteem are appreciated, his defensiveness will diminish. In other words, your efforts to enhance his self-esteem will lead to rapport between you. He will begin to view both you and himself differently, to feel better, and to mobilize his resources.

I recall two families, each having a rather incorrigible boy who seemed quite negativistic and resistent to any form of intervention. Both sets of parents had been through the mills of therapists, counselors, and juvenile services departments. In various ways their inadequacies as parents had been pointed out or alluded to. They felt, with some accuracy, that they were being blamed for their child's maladjustment. Of course, to some extent such blame would also have some accuracy. These parents exhibited the common characteristics of marital conflict involving the child and of erratic and inconsistent discipline methods, in particular the pattern of very harsh penalties impulsively handed down and then not enforced. Further, their methods and requirements constantly shifted, since nothing they tried "worked"—that is, nothing corrected their adolescent's misbehavior permanently; after a few weeks of "behaving," another problem arose and more disciplinary efforts were necessary. The parents also exhibited the not uncommon patterns of overt resistance to and apparent inability to profit from the various forms of counseling to which they had been exposed. Both sets of parents were close to family crisis. The two children were somewhat different, however. The first boy had lesser offenses of a somewhat more recent onset, while the second boy had a long history of a variety of problems and offenses.

My work with these cases consisted of brief interviews with the parents and their boy. Primarily my attention was on the two parents, and I had minimal interaction with the boy. My focus was on the parent's self-image. Using the techniques of crisis intervention, I elicited their sense of frustration and failure as parents. I sympathized with the stress they had undergone and mentioned the difficulty involved in raising teenagers under the best of circumstances. I noted that they were doing their best, how frustrating it was when their efforts did not succeed, and how concerned they were about their son's welfare. I noted that while it was only a few more years until their son was grown and on his own, a few more years of what they had all (here I included the boy) been going through could seem like a long time. All of these comments were made in the course of a dialogue rather than a monologue. I closed by noting that while people generally found it easy to blame parents, there was no simple instruction manual for parenting, largely because no one really knows how to go about it and because there are some problems that no one really knows how to solve. Both sets of parents seemed to accept these comments and to leave in a somewhat relieved state.

I do not have good followup on these two cases, but it is my understanding that in the first case the situation gradually improved somewhat, with the parents functioning somewhat more effectively, while in the second case the boy continued to get into moderately serious trouble, perhaps slightly worse, while the parents functioned about the same or slightly better. In both cases the immediate semicrisis state seemed to be resolved.

My interpretation of these events is that in a semicrisis, I practiced semicrisis intervention, focusing primarily on two points—modifying the parents' self-image, which was that of being failures—and conveying my perception of the situation—that it was relatively hopeless, there was nothing they could do. To the extent that I was successful in these goals, I believe the pressure and the onus on the parents was reduced. The parents were able to relax a bit, reduce flailing about that was making things worse, diminish some of the general hostility and blaming, and perhaps even function a bit more effectively.

I have used a somewhat similar approach in a few ongoing psychotherapy cases, in which I think I helped the parents endure for a while and reduce the pressure of their frantic efforts, while they waited for their teenager to grow up a little bit. This is not an ideal approach, and it can promote difficulties if the teenager's real need is for intervention.

However, in my experience, the fact that a teenager *needs* intervention does not necessarily mean that intervention is possible. Sometimes you have to settle for doing what you can, and sometimes just supporting the parents' self-image has some value. It is my impression that many of our rather standard approaches to dealing with juvenile problems directly assault the parents' self-image ("You did it all wrong; now change your entire personality, just dump all your neurotic hangups, readjust your internal and family dynamics, and from now on do it like this.").

Although I'm referring mostly to parents here, these comments can be applied more generally—for example, to marriage counseling. Advice, quick teaching, and simple directions on how to change one's approach to a proper one assume that the client's problem is simply ignorance and disregard the power of internal and system problems and of homeostatic forces. Nonetheless, this approach can be helpful at times. It takes a certain self-confidence, self-acceptance, and secure self-image to be able to really look at one's problems and mistakes. These directive educational approaches, such as Parent Effectiveness Training courses,* can be quite useful when these assets are present. Even then, it is difficult to make changes and to "remember" to apply what's been learned (I still reread the chapter on active listening in *P.E.T.* about every six months). However, if the ideas work, the benefits will reinforce them, and they can eventually become incorporated into one's system.

Now, I think these educational or directive methods can have some benefit even in families where the immediate problems are more serious and the parents' self-image worse. However, I think it is difficult to use such an approach in these cases, since it demands extreme care in the manner of presentation, requires much work specifically aimed at raising parental self-esteem, and takes a long time.

It should be fairly clear that I don't think these directive educational approaches will suffice in crisis intervention. In fact, I think they will assault the client's self-image and proba-

*T. Gordon, *P.E.T.: Parent Effectiveness Training* (New York: Peter H. Wyden, 1970).

bly will make things worse. When people are using their energy to protect themselves from your wise, concerned, well-intended efforts to point out their errors and failures, they're not in a position to learn much from you. Finally, there certainly are situations in which exploration of dynamics and confrontation with behavior and its underlying dynamics are indeed indicated—but *not* in crisis intervention, where the overriding principle must be protecting the client's self-image.

Self-Reliance

Each of us has a tendency to regress, that is, to retreat from a mature type of functioning to more immature styles. For example, when a child's mother has a baby, the first child may lose his toilet training and may revert to thumb sucking; when I am depressed, I may sleep more and eat more rather than directly tackling the underlying problem. Under stress we wish for the magical mother who can kiss it and make it well, who understands how we feel without our needing to say a word, who knows all the answers, and who can take care of anything. The client in a crisis has struggled and is at the end of his rope. When he finally gives in and calls for your help, he may be tempted to let go and just fall into your lap. This tendency must be actively combated from the first. Otherwise, the eventual result will be great hostility toward you for failing to deliver the magic (since you must ultimately fail), lowered self-esteem of the client because of his having been so dependent, and a worsening of the situation due to the client's continuing immobilization.

To combat this, you must make it clear that you don't know all the answers. You avoid magical reassurance ("I know this will all work out."). You give support only as indicated, and you expect effort from the client. You make sure that the client is actively doing things and is doing them with some success. Thinking in terms of action—tasks, goals, and steps—helps facilitate this process of fostering self-reliance and combating dependency.

You offer the client a chance to form a team with you, to engage in mutually assessing the situation and in planning.

The client's ideas are elicited and incorporated even if you need to fudge ("From what you said, it sounds like you're wondering if calling somebody at school, like maybe the vice-principal, might help. Were you thinking about asking how Johnny's reading really is?"). This can be said if there was the faintest hint of any such notion in what the client said. If this maneuver requires stretching it pretty far, some clients will be aware of your manipulation and some will resent it. Most appreciate your efforts to protect their self-esteem and become more comfortable with you. Their involvement in *their* plan not only increases the chance of their productively following through but also is important in fostering self-reliance.

Some clients are continually in a state of dependency, always seeking the magic mother. This, of course, is not crisis but equilibrium. Those clients can be worked with (sometimes) but not by crisis intervention. One way to check for the possibility of such chronic dependency is to ask about involvement with other workers in the past. You may then hear of a number of workers and agencies, most in terms of their inadequacies and failures to provide (although a few may be described in glowing terms). Then it is a good bet that before long you too will fall into the inadequate and failing group, no matter what you do.

A basic principle for fostering self-reliance is to do for the client nothing that he can successfully do for himself. For example, if you think he will do it successfully, have him phone for information or an appointment, even if you could do it more easily yourself.

All of this attention to the self-reliance principle will combat the regressive tendencies and thus support the self-image and foster the mobilization of the client's own efforts.

After this review of principles, it may now be fairly clear why I say that crisis intervention is not therapy—at least it is not the kind of analytically based dynamic psychotherapy that I practice. I am certainly not against therapy, but this book is about crisis intervention, and the two are different. By *therapy*, I mean a fairly extended process that establishes an intense and ongoing relationship, with encouragement of expressing and exploring feelings and fantasies in depth, with a major subgoal of insight as the means to the major goal of effecting some basic changes in the personality and some significant changes in behavior. By *family therapy,* I mean a somewhat similar process with a goal of significant changes in family patterns. I could call crisis intervention a special type of therapy, but I prefer to emphasize the distinction. The goals are different. The duration is different. Many of the techniques are different, or are applied in a different way or for a different purpose. I emphasize this point because many workers, especially those with counseling or therapy experience, have a tendency to slip into therapy when they are intending to do crisis intervention. Some workers subconsciously regard crisis intervention as a temporary process, something to do until the clients can begin, or can be coerced into beginning, psychotherapy. Some clients will indeed proceed from crisis intervention into therapy, but most won't, and if this is consciously or subconsciously the goal, there will likely be not only failure to achieve it but also failure at the crisis intervention.

At the end of this chapter on principles of crisis intervention, I repeat an important sentence: "You are attempting to convey by your entire approach your attitude that the client is a capable, decent person who has been temporarily overwhelmed by extreme stresses, and who will use your help to cope with these stresses and get back on the track." Let's dissect this sentence: "convey by your entire approach"— better than conveying it verbally; "is a capable, decent person"—supporting the self-image; "temporarily overwhelmed"—by the definition of crisis, it will be temporary—this idea provides hope and expectation; "who will use your help to cope"—defining your role (he will cope with your help; you can't cope for him, but you can offer your support to his problem solving); "get back on the track"—the goal of returning to equilibrium.

This sentence, containing many of the core concepts of crisis intervention, presents an attitude. This attitude can be deliberately cultivated, and it will be most useful as a guiding force for the worker's actions during the actual intervention.

Chapter Three

Beginning the Intervention: Establishing Communication and Rapport

Eight principles of crisis intervention were discussed in Chapter Two. These principles are guidelines for all phases of the process of intervention. That process will tend to unfold in a logical manner, especially if the worker's efforts are organized into a series of steps. The seven steps of crisis intervention, described in the remainder of this book, provide an orderly, organized plan for approaching the intervention process. Coordinated with the principles, these steps allow the worker to conceptualize a direction for the interview and the purpose of each of his maneuvers. Naturally, the separation of these steps is somewhat schematic; during the work, each separate maneuver will serve multiple purposes and bear on several of the steps at the same time. Thus, the worker does not complete one step before proceeding to the next, but he must concentrate the major part of his attention on each in its turn. Nonetheless, the steps listed below suggest a natural, orderly flow in the work and provide direction for the worker's thinking and approach:

Step 1: establishing communication and rapport
Step 2: assessing the problem
Step 3: assessing resources and strengths
Step 4: formulating a plan
Step 5: mobilizing the client
Step 6: closing
Step 7: following up

The techniques to be discussed are specific maneuvers that can facilitate the work at the various stages. Each technique is discussed in conjunction with the particular step at which it is most useful, with an explanation of when, why, and how to use it. The main techniques presented are active listening, plussing, paradox, tasks, role playing, bargaining, and anticipatory planning. They have wide application beyond crisis intervention, and most are familiar tools. However, the discussion here will focus on their specific application to the process of crisis intervention. The technique of active listening is presented first because use of this valuable tool is such an integral part of "establishing communication and rapport," the first step, that it should be understood before considering the steps.

Active Listening

"Active listening" is a term and a technique that I have borrowed from Thomas Gordon's book, *P.E.T.; Parent Effectiveness Training* (New York: Peter H. Wyden, 1970). Although I don't agree with everything that Gordon says in *P.E.T.*, it is a very good book, useful in dealing with my own kids and in helping clients with theirs, and I frequently recommend it. Here, I will discuss active listening as a technique, first with a parent-child focus, where the basic concept is most easily clarified, and then with worker-client examples as part of crisis intervention.

Active listening is not an especially new technique. Something like it is taught to most people who enter counseling-type work. However, I do not think it is usually taught in a clear and organized fashion or with a clear presentation of the basic ideas that underlie the technique. Gordon presents it in an especially clear and well-thought-out way. This is important, because while the idea seems deceptively simple, it is actually hard to understand and even harder to apply.

Active listening is based on understanding that communication between two people is a difficult process—we frequently do not say what we mean, understand someone else's meaning, or realize that we do not understand. Active listening entails listening for the latent, underlying, coded message and then checking to see if you've gotten it correctly.

Client: It's a waste of time.

Active listener: You feel kind of hopeless, and you doubt if it's worth going on.

Child: I'm not going to that dumb school anymore.

Active listener: You're really disgusted with school.

In the second example, note the difference between the decoding comment and some other possibilities—"Oh, yes you are, young man!", "What have you done now?", or even "What's bothering you?" To follow the rest of this conversation:

Child: Yeah, that dumb old lady Murphy is always picking on me.

Active listener: It's not the *whole* school that disgusts you, but you're really having a hard time with Miss Murphy.

Child:	Yeah, she always picks on me, for nothing at all.
Active listener:	Seems like she's always on your back.
Child:	Today she yelled at me 'cause I spilled some ink.
Active listener:	You had an accident and she got mad.
Child:	Yeah, I got some on Becky's dress, and she was crying and said she'd tell her mother I did it on purpose.
Active listener:	Becky was mad at you, too. Seemed like everybody was mad at you.
Child:	I bet her mom's really sore. She may not give me any more rides to skating.
Active listener:	You're afraid Becky's mom is mad, too, and that might really leave you in a jam.
Child:	Yeah. You know, I was wondering what if I called Becky's mom and explained to her, you know?
Active listener:	You think that might help.
Child:	Yeah. Well, so long, Pop.

Throughout this conversation, the adult has asked no questions; even his last statement ended with a period. It is easy to imagine the responses you might have made, and all the responses the active listener did *not* make.

Gordon lists twelve responses that we usually make to our children, and he calls these the "Terrible Twelve." These responses include such reactions as criticizing, blaming, questioning, advising, and encouraging. These responses stifle initiative, lower self-esteem; and eventually kill communication. Some examples are:

"You must have done something to her."
"Why did you do that?"
"Wouldn't it be better if you . . . ?"
"That's no way to . . . ."
"I'm sure that she doesn't really dislike you."
"I'm sure that it will all work out."

These Terrible Twelve are clearly differentiated from active listening, which consists of *only* listening and *only* checking the accuracy of the *decoded* message. It does not consist of repeating back what was said or repeating the last few words; it requires more *actively* listening, more empathy, and more imagination than that. It is also not passive listening, which Gordon describes as using those passive comments and voices that encourage more talking: "Uh huh," "Oh?", "Go on," "Yeah?", and "Mmm?" Passive listening is useful, and it's preferable to the Terrible Twelve, but it's not as useful as active listening.

Here's another example of active listening:

Child: [to Mother, slaving over a hot stove] Isn't dinner ready yet?
Mother: You're getting pretty hungry.
Child: No, I just wanted to tell Tommy what time to come over.
Mother: Oh, we'll probably get started about 7:30.

These several examples show that the active listener doesn't put her own ideas or suggestions into her responses. For example, the suggesting response to "Isn't dinner ready yet?" might be "Why don't you get a couple of cookies?" You can easily imagine other responses from the Terrible Twelve: "Can't you ever wait?", "Don't worry, it won't be long," or, "If you'd eaten your lunch like I told you, you wouldn't be so hungry now."

The comment "Oh, we'll probably get started about 7:30" is also distinct from the Terrible Twelve: "Why don't you tell him to come about eight?" or "Don't you have a lot of homework?"

Notice particularly the following:

1. Most of the active listener's responses are comments about "you," that is, the speaker, and frequently involve the listener's guess about feelings.
2. The responses are not just a feedback of the speaker's

statement but involve the listener's guess as to the *meaning* of the statement.

3. The active listener may easily be wrong, which is no great problem, since the active listening process helps correct that.

4. The active listener doesn't ask questions. He puts more of himself into the interchange than that ("I have listened carefully to you and am trying to really tune into you and how you feel and how you see things, and this is what I heard."). Questions, even tactful, considerate ones, provoke too much feeling of the naughty child being interrogated by the principal ("Why did you do that?") or having to justify himself ("How can you possibly think that?"). For many adolescents, any question is experienced immediately as an intrusion into his privacy if not as a direct accusation.

Active listening provides a number of benefits. It provides a child or a client with a chance to develop his own strengths. The process leaves the problem fully in his lap but may help him in thinking it out and working out his own solutions. This is an ego-strengthening process, which enhances self-respect and self-confidence. At the same time, it provides the talker a sense of support, of your being there with him. It also reduces interference from the talker's reactions of passivity, negativism, resentment, or sabotage— whatever his reactions are to the situation in which he is in a child role to an "authority." The active listening process conveys respect and acceptance. It conveys the attitude of expecting the client to be able to handle his problem. It develops a sense of security from criticism or ridicule and from intrusion or domination. When you practice active listening, the talker feels understood and is encouraged to talk more.

All of these facts about active listening make it a useful technique and particularly suited to our primary use for it. It may be used at various points throughout crisis intervention work, but it is not the only approach we use. It is used primarily at the beginning of the intervention process as an excellent approach for establishing communication and rapport—for helping the clients to begin talking with you in a useful way while becoming more comfortable and feeling more confident and secure with you, and for establishing an alliance relationship.

Active listening is a specific technique to be used at appropriate times and for specific purposes. Obviously, it is of most use when someone has a problem, though our examples show it is not limited to that. Active listening is not a panacea, and it must be used with some discretion. Like everything else, of course, it doesn't always work. Some clients will have adverse reactions to active listening, in which case it should be dropped, as with any other approach that isn't working. Sometimes the technique would be clearly inappropriate, as in these instances:

Son: Where's the keys, Pop?

Father: [definitely *not* active listening] I told you, you couldn't have the car tonight if you came in late again, and I'm sticking to it.

Client: Where's the bathroom?

Worker: [unfortunately trying active listening] You want to go to the bathroom.

Active listening seems deceptively simple to most people, yet it is difficult to apply. Most of us tend to slip automatically into the Terrible Twelve without even being aware of it. It is difficult to really listen, to really hear, to really understand what the other person means. Most people find that the other types of responses keep creeping in unnoticed, or they merely repeat the talker's words, or they can't think of anything to say. A good way to learn is to practice with a colleague, taking turns presenting a problem. After a few minutes, the presenter can coach the active listener as to how he was doing. Some of the difficulties in active listening are expressed in the following report, disguised but unedited, by a crisis intervention student:

Mark T is fourteen years old and has lived in foster care since age three. The past four years he has spent with one foster family and this is his surrogate family. He knows of his natural family through regular, albeit infrequent, contact; but he never had the opportunity to get to know them. His family has worked with Social Services for nine years. Their life is a struggle against the overwhelming aspects of everyday life; the parents have serious problems and are ineffectual. On 2/12/77, Mark, through much of his own effort and longing, was returned to his family: Mother, Father, twelve-year-old sister. On 2/17/77, Mark, whom I never saw before, came to my office to talk. He'd had a disastrous return home, ending in physical and verbal battling with everyone at home. He has been no problem in foster care, so he was trying to re-place himself. His father had threatened him with court, using my name. He came to talk about court and his confused situation.

I took this opportunity, for myself and Mark, to active listen. Although he made good sense to me and appeared capable, my overwhelming sensation became that of my own personal vulnerability. I was not in control and, as we plunged deeper into his feelings, I felt desperately distant from neat resolution. I literally fought the urge to quickly refer him to his social worker. This surprised me because I've active listened before, but not so totally without the urge to manipulate. *He* talked; *he* did the work; *he* resolved some of the stresses confronting him and left my office capable of confronting those yet ahead.

I gave him some info: No, he wasn't going to court or training school. I active listened and rapport did quickly grow. I plussed: shifted to relevant positive past events. I gave him my card with an open and unqualified invitation to contact me, though, by then, I felt he wouldn't need to do

so. He contacted his former foster parents and
was going to visit them for the weekend. He
accepted his position as an outsider to his family
and the pain this caused him and the confusion
this threw into his life. He left me to go to his
social worker to work towards formal replace-
ment. I supported his plans, which were sensible
and feasible. We *both* progressed: he was firmly
resolute, I was exhausted, but more educated.

Active listening sometimes takes a little time—it is easier
to turn off a child by giving him good advice and thus shorten
the conversation. Active listening means bearing some tension
as you watch someone else do his own struggling with his own
problem. It also means taking a chance that by opening
communication, you will hear something you don't like or feel
uncomfortable. And, like most other things that pay off, active
listening can be hard work.

The preceding report was a good example of a crisis
intervention completed in one session (although the boy had
more work to do on his own) and of using active listening as
the primary problem-solving mechanism. I think it worked so
well due to a combination of factors, including this worker's
skill, the boy's strength, and the fact that the boy probably
wasn't yet in full crisis and so was still functioning fairly
effectively. Of course, many cases will not respond this rapidly
or without a more complex intervention. Yet one should be
alert to such positive potential and ready to enhance progress
whenever a client is showing response. In most cases, work
must be done to clear away obstacles and provide mobilization
before clients start to move.

When active listening is used *extensively* in the beginning
of a session or when it is used later in the work, it is frequently
employed as a way to deal with emotion. The technique allows
emotion to be expressed, to be ventilated and defined, in a
controlled and nonescalating manner. The following example
is from the middle of a session:

Mother: He's a terrible boy.
Worker: You don't see much good in him.

Mother: It's not that, he's got some good points, but he won't use them. He hangs out with that crowd, he comes in late, he smokes and I know he's drinking, and . . . .

Worker: [interrupting] You worry about him a lot, and about what he's doing.

Johnny: Yeah, she worries all the time. She's always on my back about something.

Worker: Just a minute, Johnny, you think your mother over-does the worrying, and we want to hear how it looks to you in a minute, but right now let me hear what your mother's saying. [To Mother] You were saying you do worry a lot.

Mother: Yes, I do. I've talked and talked to him till I'm blue in the face, and it does no good. He just ignores me.

Worker: Your efforts just don't seem to get you anywhere.

Mother: No. Sometimes I wonder where I went wrong.

Worker: When you think of all these things that worry you, you even wonder if you're failing as a mother.

Mother: Yes. I've tried, but I must be doing something wrong. Maybe there's some other way.

In this example, the worker has dealt with the feelings in a very specific way, that is, by consistently actively listening. We see the feelings shifting from Mother's rage at her son, with the critical attacking, through her guilt-provoking self-pity ("Where have I failed"), to a somewhat less emotional and less defensive "I must be doing something wrong." This opens the door to begin looking, in a less emotional atmosphere, at what Mother has tried and what other options are available. The worker has not defended the boy, which would just increase Mother's anger and defensiveness, but has not actually sided with her anger or even quite accepted that the boy is actually doing what she says. Instead, the worker has focused on the mother's feelings and perceptions in a very accepting way. This has not alienated the boy, and the worker's reflecting process and the shifting have helped prevent the mother's statements from inflaming the boy in the session. At the same time, she feels listened to and understood.

In crisis intervention, active listening is most useful early in the session. It helps the client start talking, and it helps build rapport. Further, it is a way to handle emotions—to allow ventilation without escalation and to begin the shift toward thinking. It sets an atmosphere of respect and courteous listening in which the problem remains the client's. It can be useful later in the session to facilitate talking, enhance rapport, handle emotions, or reinforce the atmosphere. I occasionally even use it briefly just to stall for time if something comes up that I can't immediately handle.

Establishing Communication and Rapport

I believe it was the famous family therapist Virginia Satir who said that the primary goal in the first session of therapy is to leave the client willing to return for a second. The same principle applies in crisis intervention, although a second session is sometimes not necessary. To reach this goal, the worker must ensure that the client feels that something useful has been accomplished in the first session and that there is promise of something useful being accomplished in the next.

The client is fearful of certain dangers that he believes might occur in the sessions. He's fearful of explosion and loss of emotional self-control. He's fearful of self-exposure or of disclosures that might weaken his position with others. He's fearful of possible disruption of important relationships and of losing self-esteem. He is also quite aware of the price of the session, in terms of money, anxiety, and trauma. So, for him to be willing to return, he must feel that the degree of need and the potential gains justify the risk and the price. The essential foundation for the above to occur is a simple one—the formation of a positive relationship between the client and the worker.

Work on the relationship is begun in the worker's first contact with the client, which is frequently a phone call. In the first phone call, I try to obtain enough information to partially assess the situation: Is this a crisis? How urgent is it? Is this an appropriate meeting? Who shall be seen? Is any other information needed before the first session? I try to conduct this brief conversation in such a way that the client feels I'm interested in him, so that my request that he brings certain other people with him makes some sense to him, and so that some bond is formed between us. The client has been listened to. He has experienced something of my style—my listening, my questions, and a few brief comments—so that he has some idea of me and of what working with me might be like. It is the unknown and our fantasies about it that frighten us the most, so by this first brief contact some of the client's fears and fantasies have been reduced, and perhaps some misconceptions corrected. In addition, I have gained enough information to formulate a *very* tentative idea about the problem and to make some rough plans for the first meeting. As long as I can be flexible and open-minded, these premature hypotheses can be of real benefit, because I won't have to walk into the meeting totally cold and try to be spontaneously ingenious while drowning in a sea of unfamiliar data.

I do try to stay in control of this first conversation: I ask the client for a brief description of the problem and I offer some emotional support if necessary, but I do not want him to unload the entire story and all his feelings before the first session. Otherwise, he'll be disappointed when I don't give solutions immediately. Also, when the first session begins, he may have lost the desire to talk, I'll not be able to be spontaneous, and the others at the session may feel at a disadvantage. There will be a deadness and a sense of absurdity in the rehashing, and I'll have lost the opportunity to work with, direct, and modify the material as it unfolds. The idea is to establish contact, get the necessary information, and get out, leaving the rest for the session.

This first contact, with the early establishment of a slight bond, can be critical. I usually make my own appointments by telephone, so a call is the initial contact. If someone else has given the client an appointment to see me, I will usually call the client in advance and confirm the appointment. This gives me the opportunity to perform this early work. There have been studies showing that this simple calling-to-confirm procedure will markedly reduce the percentage of first-appointment no-shows, which is quite high in most clinics and agencies.

Obviously the intervention process depends on communication, and the worker tries hard to make it easy and comfortable for the clients to talk. However, it is not just talk that is desired, but useful talk. Establishing good communication is an important part of creating the desired atmosphere. This is a large and complex topic, but some principles of good communication are as follows:

1. People speak one at a time. Each speaker is listened to attentively, with the aim of understanding his viewpoint. There are occasional questions or feedback to check for accuracy of understanding.
2. People speak for themselves and not for others. Assumptions about another person's thoughts or feelings are checked out with that person.
3. Clear differentiation is made between thoughts and feelings and between facts and opinions.
4. Vague or all-encompassing generalities are not left standing, but specifics are spelled out.
5. Differences in opinion and viewpoint can be sharpened and clarified rather than just argued. If they're unresolvable, they are noted and dropped. They can sometimes just be left alone.
6. People can speak without being interrupted, but there are dialogues rather than monologues.
7. Everyone present is included in the conversation in some way, and everyone gets an opportunity to speak.

It is the worker's job to facilitate and maintain good communication and also to serve as a model of good communication to the family. This greatly facilitates the whole intervention process.

Before discussing the first session, I should emphasize

that I am describing how *I* do crisis intervention. This is not *the* way—this is *my* way, and it may or may not fit someone else. It can probably be used by most people with modifications, as each worker must adapt approaches to fit his own personal style. Though someone else may even develop an entirely different approach, he must still deal with the same issues, and the same principles will apply. These are my ways of applying them.

I begin the first session using three procedures to help establish communication and rapport: (1) taking charge, (2) monitoring anxiety, and (3) setting the atmosphere.

These procedures are so interrelated that it is difficult to discuss them separately, but I will try to do so, indicating some of the intermeshing as I go.

Taking Charge. Taking charge is an essential part of the first session in crisis intervention. It is essential that the worker control the course of the session, maintain good communication, control the level and expression of hostility, prevent undue pressure or trauma for any individual, and control both the individual level and the general level of anxiety. One of the sources of the clients' anxiety is the fear that no one will be in control and that things will get out of hand, resulting in chaos and damage. Establishing that the worker is in charge and that he will not allow undue trauma serves both to reduce the anxiety level and also to increase rapport and facilitate open communication. Because of these fears and anxieties, there very likely will be testing in the session to determine exactly who is in charge. This testing may be subtle, or it may become an overt power struggle. The worker must be prepared to meet this challenge and win.

Taking charge begins when I invite the clients into my office and courteously give them permission to be seated. These simple procedures immediately establish that I am in charge. I then give a brief explanation of the session: "I'm Dr. Puryear. I work with families when there are problems, so when Mrs. Thompson called I asked her to invite all of you to come in. We'll meet probably about an hour today. I like to see everyone together, at least at first."

Thus I have been courteous and have shown respect

and consideration by giving an explanation; I have lowered their anxiety by giving a hint of what to expect; and I have demonstrated that I know what I'm about *and* that I'm in charge.

Then I meet each person: "Your name is? And how old are you, Tommy? What grade are you in? How's it going? OK? Does that mean you're only failing half your courses or that you're on the honor roll? What kind of things do you like to do?" For the adults, I might ask their occupation, hobbies, and interests or where they come from. I've frequently formed some rapport with a relatively nonverbal working father by asking more details about his job and expressing some recognition of his knowledge, skills, or endurance. But before I go too far into anything with any one person, I make sure I've met everyone. Choosing who to start with is a separate topic, but I generally think it enhances communications if I don't start with the parents or the "culprit."

By meeting each person, I establish a relationship with each; show that I respect each of them as an important individual with something to say; lower anxiety by starting with easily answered, nonstressful questions; demonstrate that I want good communication with specific factual answers— and show that I determine who speaks and when. Thus, I have established that I am in charge. The issue is not settled there, however, attention to it must be maintained throughout the session. Challenges may arrive at any point.

It becomes particularly clear that I am in charge when someone tries to interrupt, because, in the interest of good communications, I stop them. A striking example is the impeccably dressed, poised, well-mannered matron who politely and sweetly asks, "Excuse me, Doctor, but may I interrupt for a moment?", to which I of course reply, "No, I want to hear what Joanie is saying." This is often an unusual experience for the matron and her family, producing a startled reaction and establishing that I am in charge. It may also gain me a few allies, including possibly the matron, who gazes at me with new respect.

Although I do not allow the clients to interrupt, I, of

course, must occasionally do so: "No, Mike, I can see you're just busting to say something, but I want John to finish and then I'll come to you. If you can hold it in, I'll see that you get a chance to say everything you want before we stop. OK?" This is a fairly lengthy statement and thus a lot of attention on a mildly hyperactive boy, but it is usually effective, although it may need repeating. The use of active listening is evident in the first part of the statement. If Mike couldn't hold it long, I would see to it that he got a chance to speak soon—but it would clearly be when I offered it, not when he interrupted.

It is important not to allow one person to go into a long monologue, as others will lose interest, the flow of the session will cease, and the monologuer will gain control. I might interrupt a monologue to clarify a point or, better yet, to check for confirmation or for reaction from another family member—another good communications technique. This breaks up the monologue and keeps me in charge:

"Excuse me a minute, Dad. John, Dad thinks you're mad a lot of the time. What do you think?"

"Excuse me a minute, Dad. John, you just shook your head when Dad said you've got a lot of friends."

"Excuse me a minute, Dad. John, have you ever had the kind of stomachache that Dad gets?"

"Excuse me, Dad—now that was in 1954, two years before John was born?"

"Excuse me, Dad, but you're bringing up so many good ideas I'm having trouble keeping up with them. Could we go back to what you said about John and school?"

Breaking up monologues is especially important to slow down the escalation of feelings when a monologuer is working himself up, usually in anger, or when he may be agitating someone else. Once I've interrupted and asked my question or clarified the point, I try to determine whether the speaker can tolerate giving up the floor. If he has had trouble accepting my interruption or if he still seems under great pressure to continue, I will return the conversation to him. I may say, "I see, now please go on." By giving this direction, I reinforce the fact that I am giving the orders and controlling the flow. Of course, I will continue to interrupt and will shift speakers as soon as possible. If the monologuer does not seem so hell-bent on continuing, I may further break up the monologue by asking for the viewpoint or reaction of another person to some point that the speaker has brought up. I will then go on from there rather than returning the floor to the monologuer.

People do not always respond to my first polite "excuse me." I repeat it louder and, if necessary, louder yet. I then make it quite clear that I'm no longer listening. I shout "Excuse me!" and stand up. If necessary, I will slam my hand down on the table. I've rarely had to go this far, but when I do, I'll usually apologetically explain that for this work I must be able to interrupt when I need to ask a question. Or, I might just say, "Excuse me, but I wanted to ask . . . ." I've never had to go further than the hand banging. I think that if that didn't work, I would just leave the room and return a little later with an explanation. On occasion, if it's been slightly hard to interrupt, if I seem to have offended someone, of if someone has pointed out that I interrupt but don't give them the same privilege, then I apologize and explain that while it's important for clear communication that they not interrupt, it's essential for the way I work that I be able to. Then I ask their permission to keep this privilege. I've not yet been refused, and so we proceed. Once someone does not respond to my "excuse me," the resolution of who's in charge takes precedence; whatever is being said is temporarily ignored.

Another useful method of taking charge is "drawing a line." I stumbled on this one day while dealing with an overbearing, domineering father who seemed to be running the interview more than I was. At one point he said, "Now, I know what you're thinking, Doctor, you're thinking that I believe Jane's boyfriend is no good just because he has long hair, and . . . ." At that point I burst in with "Excuse me, Mr. Jones, but let's get one thing clear. I may tell you what I'm thinking, or you can tell me what you think I'm thinking, but *you* don't tell *me* what *I'm* thinking!" He sat back for a moment, said "OK," and apologized; the rest of the interview went beautifully.

On rare occasion I have deliberately drawn other lines, such as "Let's be clear, there will be no profanity used in this office!" (useful only when I haven't been using profanity already in that session) or "There will be no feet on the furniture!" (useful only if I haven't had my feet on the furniture). Again, the sole point is to maintain myself being in charge. I use some care in the above maneuvers; even more than with most maneuvers, I try to apply them only in situations where I feel they will work. It is hard to recover after taking such a position if it does not work.

There is a special type of situation in which I have felt nothing would work. Someone storms in ready for a fight and is by God going to have his say. In those situations I have used "sitting it out." I took the position that I wanted to be perfectly clear about *his* position. I listened attentively, made a few notes, and sometimes, when there seemed to be a slight opening, asked a brief clarifying question ("Excuse me, was that this week or last week?"). On occasion, the speaker will attempt to pull me in more. One father once asked, "Wouldn't you feel the same way if it were your son?" In this instance I had a chance to maintain a little control and establish my position more clearly: "I'd rather go ahead and get clear about your position on this. Go on please." I've used this about three times, and each time the person ran down in less than half an hour. Depending on the situation, it may then be possible to move on to some work. Otherwise, a worker can just close the session. So, while I relinquish control when I sit it out, by giving the person permission to take over, I ultimately remain in charge.

Monitoring Anxiety. By *monitoring anxiety,* I mean to be aware of the anxiety level in the room and in each individual *and* to regulate that level. I do not undertake the impossible task of eliminating anxiety—even if that could be done, it would markedly reduce the client's motivation to work on problems. But I do try to keep the anxiety within tolerable limits, so that no one is too uncomfortable and so that the session does not become too unpleasant. In regulating anxiety, I find that I must particularly try to regulate the amount of emotion generated and expressed and how the emotion is expressed. This applies to hostility in particular. In crisis intervention sessions, it is most often hostility that boils up enough to interfere with the work.

There are many indicators of anxiety level—nervous movements, foot tapping, pressured speech, silence, shifting topics, chain smoking, and so on. I note these indicators as they occur as well as noting another good indicator—the degree of tension within myself. Of course, I try to assess the source of my own tension, but frequently such tension reflects the general anxiety level in the session. Sometimes the anxiety is quite obvious and sometimes it is more subtle, but it is nearly always communicated if you stay attuned to it.

The client or family usually enters the session with a fairly high level of anxiety. The first few moves of the worker should tend to lower the anxiety level. These first actions should also establish the worker as being in charge, as well as being competent; establishing these points will also tend to lower the anxiety. The family will be appreciative of the lowered anxiety, and rapport will begin to build.

The opening questions are part of getting acquainted and are nonstressful and easily answered. This breaks the ice while people are getting used to the setting and especially to the worker. Some gentle joking, especially with a child, will usually help. If it is clear that someone has walked in just bursting to talk, ready to spill it all, I will still do the get-acquainted procedures—partly to establish control—but I will keep them brief, so that the person's frustration does not become too great.

After getting acquainted, it is important to start with the family's concerns. I don't want to help scapegoat a child, but if the child is their focus and their complaint, we have to start there. To do otherwise leaves them too frustrated, and they won't be able to pay full attention to what I'm focusing on. It is better to let them ventilate, with some active listening at first, while I begin to shape, control, and modify what they're presenting. Therefore, I usually start by asking about the problem.

Occasionally, if the anxiety is quite high and particularly

if someone is not joining in, I may specifically address the anxiety. I may talk about how difficult coming to these sessions can be, how frequently people are uncomfortable at first, and so on. I may ask what they expected the session to be like. These techniques can be useful, but they don't seem to work as well for me as I'd like. Some of the other approaches to reduce and bypass the anxiety are usually more effective for me and save time by getting more directly into things and by not starting with a focus on feelings.

Also, at the onset it is always important to get each person to speak up. If someone has "no ideas" about the problem or whatever I've asked, I often take them literally. Then questions about how long they've found it safer not to have any ideas, what's it's like not to have any ideas, or what they do with an idea if they get one will open conversation. Sometimes I may just try to get an idea from them about anything and then treat that as though they've done what I wanted. If someone is evasive, saying "I see it just like he said," I reply, "Fine, now would you tell it in your own words?" As a last resort, if I'm still not getting anywhere, I will ask the family members to help out the unresponsive member. This helps get me off the hook and stay out of a power struggle.

It is important to establish that everyone talks. The exception to all of this is the overtly hostile, defiant adolescent—usually the scapegoat. His general demeanor gives advance warning. I will invite him to speak, but if I get nothing, I will quickly back off ("Maybe you don't feel like saying anything right now."). If the family tries to get him to speak, I will protect him ("I don't believe Johnny feels like talking right now."). As the session progresses, I may check with him about something requiring minimal response ("Does that sound right to you, Johnny?") and drop it, whether or not he responds. Mostly, though, I ignore him and proceed with the session as though he wasn't there—although still protecting him if necessary. In my experience, most of these teenagers begin to talk by about the middle of the session and become increasingly verbal if we don't focus too much attention or pressure on them then.

If feelings are rising during the session, especially if

hostility is expressed or if someone is being attacked too much, I will quickly intervene. The simplest way to do this is to change the subject. This is best accomplished by first sticking to the same general topic but in a less emotional way.

Mr. Jones: He never does a lick of work around the house, just lays around all day, like some damn bum.

Worker: What kind of chores does he have?

This example shows a shift away from judgmental generalities to specific facts. I ask for clarifying data and details — what chores, when did that occur, who was there, and so on. This factual information is usually not so emotionally hot — and, of course, this technique fosters good communications. It requires a little imagination to see what *not* to ask; for example, "Has he ever done this before?" opens the door for "He's always doing it!" (although that can be countered with "When was the first time?"). It would be better to start with "When was the first time?" You may cool things off further by spending several minutes really clarifying the date if desired; you then have the option of going on with the narrative or of asking, "What were things like before that?" This is a move that is really valuable in decreasing hostility — the search for "When were things better?" Frequently, after remembering the better times, people can move back into discussing the problem with much less hostility.

Obviously there are innumerable ways to change the subject, and I will only give a few more examples:

1. Ask about the process. "Do you two get this mad very often?" Then one might try to clarify this further by asking how often — "Once a day? Once a month? Well, closer to once a week or once a month?"
2. Ask for related information. "What do the kids usually do while you two are arguing?"
3. Try the direct approach. "Hey, I have some more questions to ask here — could you two hold off the arguing for a while?"

Sometimes I intervene in the proceedings by asking people to change their seats, which frequently shifts the emotional alignments in the session and facilitates shifting the process. In any event, the mechanics of shifting and the people's bewilderment at my request usually divert the process of emotional buildup. I also utilize this method to break up duos or other groupings who are so mutually involved that they are effectively staying uninvolved in the session. Of course, the process of shifting also underlines the fact that I am in charge.

Another way to tone down an emotional argument is to focus the participants' attention on the worker. This can sometimes be done merely by asking a question of one of the arguers each time they begin to talk to each other. If necessary, this can be made an experiment or a rule ("Let's try something now. For the next ten minutes I want each of you to speak only to me and to say nothing to each other. OK, John? OK, Mary?") The argument may then continue through the worker, but now the worker has a chance to modify it and tone it down.

I sometimes find it helps maintain control, prevent emotional buildup, and diminish defensiveness to use questioning in an erratic style, jumping from topic to topic. This is the opposite of good interview or good therapy technique— which tries to develop and build up feelings. Such unpredictable discussion sometimes works for me, possibly because the people can't see where I'm heading and don't get their defenses ready. A given question may be threatening, but the subject is changed again before it becomes too uncomfortable.

If all other methods fail to allay the anxiety, hostility, or general emotional buildup, then I will break up the group and ask someone or a few people to leave the room, usually not the angriest or most verbal persons. An interesting example is that of a father who repeatedly and tenaciously attacks a child verbally. Sometimes if the mother is asked out of the room, the father's approach will change dramatically. These changes in the group are made flexibly, frequently in the form of an experiment and in such a way that I can keep shifting the groupings around as I proceed.

During a session, if it becomes clear that a subject is painful or emotionally loaded, so that the clients block on discussing it, change the subject, or refuse to discuss it, I accept that. I almost never push, argue, reason, beg, or try to find other ways to draw them out. To do so usually leads to increased defensiveness, threatens the client, and tends toward a power struggle—a power struggle that I would probably lose. It certainly does not build rapport. Instead, I will move to other, less threatening matters. If necessary, I will eventually move back to the painful topic from another direction, usually as though it had never been mentioned before. This return may even be necessary more than once, but it usually produces results. Sometimes if someone shows hesitancy or reluctance about a topic, especially if they seem to be using a teasing manner ("I've something awfully important to tell you, but I don't know if I should"), I will reply, "No, please don't tell me about that unless you want to—it may be too painful right now." This usually produces the material fairly soon. If not, the topic will frequently come up or it can be inconspicuously revived later.

Setting the Atmosphere. Setting the atmosphere is one of the results of the approaches that have just been discussed. However, it also requires separate attention. The worker needs to stay in touch with the atmosphere of a session and to continually shape it toward the desired state. Atmosphere is a complex concept. It includes the psychological idea of set, the participants' expectations and perceptions of the ongoing process. Atmosphere also includes the *emotional tone,* the general feeling within the session—for example, tension, good will, humor, or hostility. It includes the sociological concept of *mores*—the group traditions, taboos, rules, and styles that are considered important, are expected to be followed, and are reinforced by group pressure.

Each family has its own mores, which include covert rules that carry great weight but are not often verbally expressed and may even be unconscious. For example, in one family, everyone's always home for Sunday dinner, they never close the doors to their bedrooms, males don't cry, Mother musn't be upset, it must be pretended that no one knows that Mary is illegitimate, and it must never be acknowledged that

Timmy is slightly retarded. Oh yes, and it must never be acknowledged that any of these rules exist.

So, the atmosphere is made up of the emotional tone, the set, and the mores *of the session.* These exert strong forces, and we want to control and use them. Whatever the family's tendencies, we will have to exert potent efforts in order to establish the atmosphere we want and need in the session. We want to control the atmosphere, because it can exert a powerful influence on the family—on their behavior with each other and with us, at least within the session. Of course, there is some hope that this setting of the atmosphere, coupled with some of the other shifts that might occur during the session, will carry over somewhat outside of the session. This is not a large hope, though, because homeostatic equilibrium is powerful. The family already has years of its traditional experiences, and they spend most of their time outside of the few brief sessions. Also, being too hopeful of change can lead us to do therapy instead of crisis intervention. Nonetheless, it is exactly during times of crisis, during great discomfort, turmoil, and disequilibrium, that some changes may occur. In this way the ideas about atmosphere and its influence fit in with the concept of equilibrium and the principle of goals. Again we encounter the paradox of secretly hoping for some long-term, deep changes and some significant growth within the family while *operating* with the limited goal of problem-solving crisis resolution.

The atmosphere desired in the session is one of cooperative teamwork in a problem-solving process. The family will bring in their current atmosphere, some of which is an expression of their state of equilibrium and some of which reflects their crisis state. Their atmosphere may contain combinations of fear, fighting, blaming, scapegoating, emotionality, and guarded withdrawal. They may operate with underlying principles of "children don't count." Since most of these elements will interfere with the problem-solving work we are trying to do, we will be striving to offset them during the session. However, we want to look for any part of the family's approach that does seem useful and to utilize it where possible. We also must not plunge into something the family just can't tolerate—if they can't talk about sex, they can't, and it will either have to be left out or, if it's crucial, approached indirectly. Also, although we may disagree with some of the parents' approaches and even may need to modify some of them for the session, we do not want to undermine their authority. Fortunately, the approach and techniques we have available, many of which have already been discussed, inherently tend to set the atmosphere in the desired way.

Here, first in general and then in more detail, is my approach to setting the atmosphere. Clearly, I want it established early that I am in charge. This is part of the atmosphere—that I am in charge and will see that no one gets hurt. My role is to be the expert in problem-solving techniques and to work as an organizer, consultant, and teammate with the family. I will be available to the family within those roles. Further, I will be the captain of the team and be responsible for what happens in the sessions—to the extent that I can be—but I am not responsible for solving the family's problems. I am respectful of each person, and therefore I respect their feelings and their viewpoints. Each person is important. Everyone gets to talk, and we will all strive for good communication. I will see to it that anxiety does not get too high and that hostility and other emotions do not get out of hand. All of this describes the atmosphere that is desired; at the same time, it describes in a general way the approach that obtains it. Each of these components of the atmosphere is spelled out in the session primarily by *doing* it, not by saying it. Both by my own example and by my attitude, by my actually guiding and influencing what happens, I will shape the atmosphere.

Some of the approach to setting the atmosphere has already been described in earlier sections, from other viewpoints. In other words, many of those earlier ideas serve multiple purposes, including setting the atmosphere. Now we will specifically examine this process.

First, I emphasize the use of a great deal of courtesy. The tension and urgency of the crisis situation, the stress and fatigue of the job, and the routine flow of clients through our lives may make us forget or disregard manners. This is especially true in an institution or an agency, which often tends to have a dehumanizing effect on workers and on clients. The worker's courtesy will have some effect on the family members—as a role model, as a way of showing what is expected from them, as a form of social pressure for them to respond in kind, and as a way of increasing rapport. This helps create an atmosphere of courteous interaction, which fosters good communication. The courtesy in itself shows the clients that they are respected, even though they may feel unworthy of respect. Also, strangely enough, courtesy assists in taking charge; for example, the simple courtesy of inviting the clients into the office and offering them (that is, giving them permission to take) a seat already indicates that you are in charge. I use courtesy throughout the interview, even when I am aggressively interrupting or drawing a line—when I shout to interrupt Mr. Jones, I shout courteously, "Excuse me, Mr. Jones!" Being courteous does *not* mean being passive, letting yourself be pushed around, or giving up control of the session.

The courtesy of meeting each person at the outset continues the process of *your* running the session and establishes some rapport; it also establishes that each individual has a valid and respected part in the proceedings. The use of active listening early in the session is an excellent way to convey respect and interest while maintaining control. You listen in a noncritical and nonjudgmental way, and this serves as a model of communication. In this process I tend, with some rare exceptions, to accept *all* feelings and viewpoints as valid—that is, they may be inaccurate, but it is a person's valid, legitimate right to have them. At the same time, I try to label them as feelings or viewpoints, as opposed to facts, at least when the client will let me get away with it ("I see, Mrs. Jones, it's your opinion that Tommy is really headed downhill into being a real alcoholic, and that's what you worry about the most.")

Consider the following exchange:

Worker: I see, Mr. Jones, you consider these various voices
                 to be messages from the Martians directly to you.
Mr. Jones: No, I don't *consider* them as messages, they are
                 messages!
Worker: I see, so you have no question in your own mind,
                 you're certain of it.
Mr. Jones: Absolutely!

There I still managed to slip in a "in your own mind,"
still suggesting that this idea represents Mr. Jones' opinion,
and this time he let me get away with it. There is a helpful
active listening quality in my comments, although this is not
truly active listening. This kind of process helps me avoid an
argument with a client and allows me to raise a slight question
about his views without directly attacking them and without
questioning his right to hold them. It serves as a model of
communication for the family of not having to argue with
someone; for example, it shows the family that they needn't
consider a different opinion as a threat that must be eradi-
cated. It also helps them to differentiate among feelings,
opinions, and facts. Tommy's hostility is reduced when he
hears his mother's statement that he's becoming an alcoholic
labeled as her opinion or her fear, instead of having it left
standing as a statement of fact. Parenthetically, if Mr. Jones
had not let me get away with slipping in "in your own mind"
but had reasserted the "facts," I would have tried to withdraw
gracefully with a comment like "I understand how you feel
about this, Mr. Jones, and though I might not see things the
same way, we won't need to argue about it. You were saying
that last week your wife was about to leave you?" Throughout
these maneuvers, the other family members will note how I
handle these matters and how I react to a difference of
opinion. They might not only use this as a model for themselves—a slight possibility, actually—but they may become
more comfortable about speaking their own minds in the
session.

Plussing is a technique that will be discussed later. It partially consists of looking for the positive in people rather than focusing on the negative. This becomes part of the atmosphere, and the technique reduces hostility and blaming. This noncritical approach encourages people to open up more. Focusing on problem solving and frequently asking questions of the right sort, with occasional references to "our work here," helps develop a desirable set of thinking and working and of problem solving.

The issue of the "right sort of questions" is an important one. Much of the time during the session, I will be asking questions, and I tend to employ a very useful process of having the family members explain things to me while I listen and occasionally ask another question in order to be sure that I am understanding them correctly: "Excuse me, Mr. Johnson, I'm getting a little confused on this point. Did you mean that when your wife called the police, you thought she wanted to get rid of you for good? Or did you mean you wrote it off as just something she was doing because she was really mad right then?" It's sometimes amazing how many issues I can raise and get considered if I ask about them rather than state or suggest them. I try to avoid threatening or blaming questions, especially the dreaded why question. The simple question "Why did you do that?" is usually heard as an accusation of incompetence at best and of deep malevolence at worst, and must generally be answered with rationalizations. This response is not semantically accurate or logical, but it is social reality. The why question is what the towering principal asks the quivering little boy. I deal with motivation issues largely through plussing and through clarifying communications ("You mean when he said that, you thought he meant he had stood you up on purpose?"). I try to avoid questions of motivation and emotion, focusing more on what questions ("What happened next?"). Good questions yield information, raise issues, and stimulate thinking: ("What have you tried that didn't work?" "What did you consider trying and decide not to try?").

Sometimes why questions seem necessary, and sometimes they aren't too bad if you can figure out an indirect way to ask them: "When you were struggling to figure out what to do next, what things did you consider that led you in that direction?" Inelegant, convoluted, awkward, yes—but not "Why?"

Thus far I have emphasized the need to diminish emotionality and, in particular, hostility. As people become more emotional, their capacity for thinking decreases. A great deal of anxiety in the session is related to pent-up emotions or, conversely, to people getting carried away by their emotions. It is important to allow controlled ventilation of emotions, especially early in the session. Also, there are those cases in which emotions—unfinished grieving, for example—are at the core of the problem. In general, I find hostility the most common emotion brought into crisis intervention, for reasons already stated. Because hostility works against the teamwork problem-solving atmosphere, it must be kept at a manageable level.

Occasionally a person comes into a session and begins to "spill his guts," issuing a tremendous outpouring of self-revelation and emotion. This must be quickly halted. Generally, the person will be embarrassed about it later and unable to return. At any rate, most of the material will be irrelevant to the crisis intervention work and interfere with it. Also, whenever one family member becomes too emotional, he may turn off the other family members, causing them to withdraw and become unavailable for the work. The worker must control this.

Sometimes the opposite problem arises. Some families will not become very involved in the session and may show an apparent minimum of hostility and anxiety. Such situations are quite rare in a true crisis situation, but they do *seem* to occur—though the assessment must be questioned. In such a situation, after going through the usual procedures, I try to generate some interaction, whether hostile or otherwise, to get something going. It rarely seems effective to try to draw the family out by reassuring or begging. Sometimes I can get something going by asking the family to discuss some issue and arrive at a family position. Sometimes I can start an argument by collecting each person's opinion on some emotional issue ("What do you see as the main problem here?") and then feeding the discrepancies back to them ("Mr. Jones, you saw the main problem as a lack of money, while Mrs. Jones thought the family's never getting together caused trouble, and Tommy thought that there is no problem in the first place. That seems to be quite a difference in viewpoints."). If that doesn't work, which is rare, I will specifically ask the clients to discuss these viewpoints and arrive at an agreement. If *that* doesn't work, I can consider making an inflammatory, nonplussing statement by innocently asking a question like "Does Johnny always give in to his dad that easily?"

These maneuvers are fraught with difficulties—if the family is so defensive and guarded, drawing them into something will threaten them. Unless you can handle whatever develops very effectively, they're liable not to come back. However, if you can't get something going, they're liable not to return anyway.

Both the concept and a set of principles of good communication have been discussed. I have been using communication in two senses. First, establishing communication refers to creating an atmosphere and a relationship in which people feel unthreatened, comfortable, free, and encouraged to communicate; second, good communication refers to following a set of communication principles that establishes an effective and efficient exchange of ideas. Communication technique refers to utilizing those principles so as to establish communication in the first sense. Good communication makes people more willing to open up in a session, thus it helps to establish communication. Because it encourages people to discuss specific facts in an orderly fashion, it facilitates problem solving.

In less direct ways, communication technique is of real assistance in setting the atmosphere—for example, it's an avenue for taking charge and it fosters attitudes of mutual respect. At the same time, both good communication and the valuing of good communication are parts of the atmosphere we try to set. In using communication technique, the worker serves as a model and also actively directs and controls communication in the session, and he sometimes actively teaches the family.

"Excuse me, Mr. Jones, but you've already brought up so many good ideas that I want to stop and be sure I've gotten some of them straight. If I try to follow too many ideas at once, I just get confused and wind up losing them." Here I am breaking up a monologue, courteously and tactfully staying in control, enhancing the client's self-esteem, and teaching him something about his style of communicating. The rest of the family is observing this interchange—they may learn something about communication, too.

Following is an example of controlling and *teaching* communication: "Excuse me, Johnny, but your dad was talking and then I couldn't pay attention to what you were saying too. I find this work goes better if I can get everyone's ideas, and that's easier to do if everyone will try to talk one at a time, OK?" Here I am handling Johnny, but I am also saying something to the whole family about interruptions.

There are some families in which chaos is the pattern and everyone talks at once routinely. Frequently no one expects to be listened to, and the verbal content is less important than the volume and the physical communication (hitting or threatening to hit). This pattern may require frequent interruptions and a great deal of traffic control to try to get the routine, the ground rules, the atmosphere of the session established. This can be quite difficult. Sometimes it can be accomplished after a while, and sometimes it requires continual effort and attention.

We want to ensure that only one person speaks at a time, and we try to increase listening. In general, we want to keep interruptions to a minimum, except our own, which are necessary. By breaking up monologues, controlling communication flow, and making sure that everyone gets a chance to speak, the realistic need of family members to interrupt is diminished ("Excuse me, Mrs. Jones; Johnny, you looked like you wanted to say something about that.").

Except when strategy dictates otherwise, the worker's statements should be brief and clear. Opinions should not be stated as fact, and that distinction should be clarified and labeled in the family's communications. Differences can sometimes be resolved by clarifying the communications; at other times the differences can be clarified, deemotionalized, and left standing:

"So, we see that you, Mrs. Jones, prefer red, as you have all your life, while you, Johnny, are partial to blue, the color of your girlfriend's eyes."

"So, Mr. Jones, here we have a definite difference; you are sure there are messages from someone controlling your thoughts, while my belief is that the noises have no significance. OK, our difference seems clear on that; tell me, when did these arguments between you and Mrs. Jones first start?"

The worker should frequently label feelings and impressions, and he should frequently check his own impressions for accuracy ("Johnny, I'm not sure I understood. Are you saying that it seems to you that Mom favors Mary and lets her do more, and sometimes you feel kind of neglected?").

Throughout the sessions, it is important to try to keep things factual and specific. This is necessary for good communication, it serves to diminish hostility and general emotionality, and it is essential for effective problem solving. Do not accept generalities or vague, broad statements, but clarify them. Sometimes this is difficult:

Mrs. Jones: He's always coming in drunk.

Worker: How often?

Mrs. Jones: All the time!

Worker: Seven nights a week?

Mrs. Jones: Most of them!

Worker: Six?

Mrs. Jones: I don't count them.

Worker: Of course not, but what's your rough guess? Is it closer to seven nights a week or closer to seven nights a month?

Mrs. Jones: Oh, closer to seven nights a week.

Worker: OK, closer to six nights a week or closer to two
                 nights a week?

Mrs. Jones: [seeing worker is serious and finally pausing to
                 think] Oh, about three or four times a week.

Worker: [who could have left it there but decides to push
                 it] OK, fine. Now this is Tuesday; let's look at the
                 past week. Last Tuesday night?

There are other specific techniques to use here. Sometimes a person just "can't guess" how many times her husband
struck her, or how many beers a day he drinks, or whatever.
Using absurdity and going to the extreme worst possibilities
are useful:

Worker: Well, of course you don't keep count, and it's
                 different in different months, but let's just get a
                 rough idea of an average month. Now, how
                 many times would you catch your wife drinking
                 with some other guy—as many as 200?

Mr. Jones: No, not 200.

Worker: Well, OK, more than 0 and less than 200. More
                 than twice?

Beyond a goal of maintaining control, the point here is
partly to get the information and partly to establish that
we will deal in specifics. This is the reason for pushing
so hard early in the session.

In some families, people only seem to pay attention
when the focus is on themselves, when the worker is conversing directly with them. Otherwise they just withdraw or turn to
someone else in the family and start another conversation. In
some other families it is the routine pattern to break into pairs
or subgroups and have several conversations going on at
once—in a more structured fashion than with chaotic families.
I find these patterns difficult to deal with, but it's important to
try to keep everyone involved:

"Mrs. Jones, I'm not sure, but I get the impression your mind is on something else right now. Could you say something about it?"

"Mr. Jones, what did you think of what your wife just said? You didn't hear it? Oh, I'm sorry. Johnny, could you repeat it for your father? You didn't hear it either? Wow— Mrs. Jones, maybe you could try speaking up. Who did hear it?"

If a family is breaking up, with a pair carrying on their own conversation, I will frequently ask the pair what they're saying or ask one of them if he heard what was just said. I'll ask for his ideas about it, after first filling him in if necessary. Sometimes I direct attention to the process and ask the family if this pairing off is characteristic, what the usual pairings are, if it's always been the same pattern, and so on. In a few cases I might ask what they think about it, but generally that sounds somewhat accusatory and isn't very productive. Sometimes I will ask the whole family to discuss some particular issue and arrive at a family answer or position. Then I sit back and watch how they proceed, which is interesting. Frequently I'll ask people to change seats to break up a particular combination. Sometimes that works very well, but sometimes the problem is not so much the particular duo or subgroup but rather that subgrouping is the family pattern; in these cases seat shifting merely leads to new subgroups.

Some of the maneuvers I have just described are more suitable to family therapy than to crisis intervention, since they tend to focus directly on the family, perhaps in a somewhat threatening manner, and shift away from the problem-solving process. Nonetheless, such maneuvers seem necessary sometimes as a way of setting the atmosphere so that the problem solving can proceed effectively.

I have emphasized the worker serving as a model for the family. This means that the family may observe how the worker functions and begin to identify with him so that they consciously or unconsciously begin to adopt some of his ways. They may respond as though the worker is illustrating alternative ways of functioning that they have never thought of or been exposed to. It is possible that this experience itself may have a continuing impact on the family outside the sessions—on their communications style, interactions, and hence relationships. I do not know how important or effective such processes are, but I think it's a bit naive to expect them to have much effect very often. I think that a social pressure process, in which the worker's manner exerts some pressure on the family to respond in kind, creates somewhat more effect during the actual session. Finally, I think that a worker who does *not* serve as a good model can have a significant deleterious effect, at least in the session.

I have discussed three procedures that are basic to the first step of establishing communication and rapport: taking charge, monitoring anxiety, and setting the atmosphere. Again, this crisis intervention approach is integrated, so that any given maneuver fits into the overall scheme in a number of ways and can serve a number of purposes. As examples, a maneuver designed to keep in charge will serve at the same time to lower anxiety and to improve communication, as when I tactfully interrupt Mr. Jones who is starting to deprecate his son. Techniques that improve communication serve at the same time to show respect for each individual and his views, as when I stop Johnny from interrupting his father and emphasize that I want to hear both of them.

As the session nears its end, I try to plan for the conclusion. Sometimes I may end with a summary of what's been discussed or a review of plans that have been made. Whatever the ending, I try to move toward less emotional and less sensitive material, and I particularly maneuver to end on a note of some positive feelings. As the final step in establishing the relationship, at the end of the first interview I always give the clients something. This may be my card with my phone number on it, a card with the names and numbers of some agencies to call, an article or pamphlet to read, pictures the children drew during the session, lollipops, or what have you. This is something that the client can physically carry out of the session and have with him until the next time. This is frankly a bit of magic, equivalent to the oldtime G.P. who always gave you a prescription for something. I believe such practice helps ensure that the clients feel that they have received something from the session and that they are cared about and valued; it helps cement a bond of relationship and support until the next contact.

Chapter Four

Maintaining a Positive Setting: Two Special Techniques

Plussing and paradox, along with active listening, are the most important special techniques used regularly throughout crisis intervention. They help to attain and maintain communication and rapport and to avoid power struggle, to raise self-esteem, and to leave the responsibility for problem solving with the client. Thus, they help to establish the desired atmosphere, and they are major factors in the fundamental style of this approach. In addition, each of these techniques is uniquely suited for dealing with certain aspects of the difficult situations that may arise.

Plussing

Plussing is a technique for enhancing a positive atmosphere in the session, for diminishing hostility, and for raising self-esteem. It is useful throughout the work but can be particularly useful in the first session to help enhance communication and build rapport. Plussing is based on assuming an attitude that people are basically good and that all actions have at least some positive or altruistic motivation. In other words, the worker deliberately plays Pollyanna.

"I see, Mr. Jones, you're so angry at Tom because you worry about him so much."

"I see, Mrs. Jones, you hit Sally because you just exploded when you thought she might be getting herself into serious trouble, and you felt absolutely helpless to stop her."

Another aspect of plussing is to focus on the positive portion of any behavioral sequence.

"So, Mr. Jones, after you wrecked the car you knew your wife was going to be worrying about you, and when you went into the bar your intention was to call her."

Even that statement could still be improved. While in therapy we generally want our patients to take more responsibility for their own behavior, in crisis intervention we are more interested in protecting self-esteem and diminishing hostility. For instance, we don't want to stimulate the family's hostility toward one family member. For those reasons, it would be better to say to Mr. Jones, "So, Mr. Jones, after the car wreck . . . ," which depersonalizes the incident. It is important to consider such things and to think about *how* we're going to say something.

People are so complex that we cannot accurately attribute any reaction or any piece of behavior to a single cause or motivation. In psychoanalytic terms, we refer to the principle of multidetermination. The id presents so many demands, so many drives clamoring for satisfaction; the superego has so many prohibitions sternly enforced and goals rigidly required; the external environment presents so many reality pressures

and consequences to be weighed; and all of these factors are
constantly bearing on the poor ego, and each must be considered. The ego is swamped with pressures and demands at any
given instant, and though one or a few of them may momen-
tarily be most apparent, seem most relevant, or appear to be
exerting the most force, a person's behavior reflects the ego
doing its best to reach some form of compromise among all of
them. The ego constantly struggles to find courses that will
gain maximal possible satisfaction of these multiple demands
while minimizing undesirable consequences.

From this viewpoint, then, with a little imagination we
should be able to dig out some useful, positive, and socially
admirable motivation behind any action. This plussing diminishes our client's defensiveness and hostility toward us; he
doesn't feel threatened by us. It enhances his self-esteem and
diminishes hostility toward him from the other family members. We are not supporting and encouraging the hostility,
and we provide the family a different viewpoint about the
behavior, which they may adopt. Plussing markedly diminishes arguing, accusing, and blaming in the session. During
the first session, active listening begins to be liberally laced
with plussing. This is no longer pure active listening, since the
worker is interjecting some of his own ideas. As the focus of
the work shifts from establishing communication and rapport
over to assessing the problem more directly ("What happened
next?"), plussing is used very liberally. During much of a
session, I plus at both subtle and at rather blatant levels—it is
inherent in the approach.

In a recent session with fourteen-year-old Randy, his
mother, his stepfather, and the other children, I noticed that
Randy frequently interrupted while I was talking with his
parents. His interruptions seemed irrelevant to the topic and
to the situation. I could handle them adequately in the session,
but they were interfering and were somewhat annoying to me,
and the parents were becoming increasingly annoyed with
Randy. I then noticed something, and after making one of my
"disclaimer" statements ("I sometimes get weird psychiatry
ideas in these sessions, but . . . ,"), I asked the parents if they'd

noticed that Randy interrupted whenever the topic of his natural father came up. They hadn't noticed this and didn't think it was true. They doubted it could be more than a coincidence. We then continued our previous discussion. However, Randy interrupted less frequently thereafter, and when he did, rather than becoming irritated, the parents checked to see whether his interruption fit (or contradicted) my "weird idea."

Now, I think my idea had some validity and some relevance to the underlying dynamics of Randy and the family. If it had been family therapy, this fact would have been quite important, and the overall issue of the natural father's place in the family—that is, in the family dynamics, even if he was not physically present—would certainly have come up again. However, this session was not family therapy but crisis intervention. So what was I doing? First, in a very indirect and somewhat awkward way, I was plussing. I clearly implied that Randy was not "a bad boy who interrupts" but "a person who is struggling with some issues and who responds in some understandable way to certain stimuli." This relabeled Randy. Now when Randy interrupted, the parents responded differently and looked at him from a different viewpoint. It is my unproven impression that if I had tried to talk to the parents about the relabeling (that Randy was not a bad boy) they would have dismissed it as a weird psychiatry idea; if I had commented on their irritation, they probably either would have denied it or taken it as an opening to launch an attack about all the ways that Randy is *always* irritating. This is another example of the value of *doing* rather than talking.

Further, one can see as plussing that I *implied* that the parents might be interested in observing and understanding such phenomena as the pattern of the interruptions, or at least that I saw them as capable of doing so. I diverted and defused the hostility that was growing in the session and interfered with the scapegoating process that was evolving. These accomplishments were more important and are more representative of the reason for my action than the actual issue of the natural father. It might have been a different situation if

The Problem were "the family has not yet adjusted to losing one member and incorporating another," but that was not the case. Finally, I did plant a seed of thought about Randy and his natural father, a seed that might have some beneficial effect later—but that is quite coincidental to the crisis intervention process.

Incidentally, I do not mean to give the impression that I had thought through all these factors and meanings before I spoke in the session. I *was* aware of trying to figure out a way to diminish the growing hostility concerning the interruptions, and more generally I was aware that the parents were viewing Randy negatively. I was also aware of my own irritation. The actual intervention I made was not the one that I might have chosen as the best possible upon later reflection, because it touched too directly on dynamics and moved away from problem solving. It revealed the interference of my dynamic therapy orientation when I am doing crisis intervention, a problem of which I have to remain aware. Yet, the intervention was not actually *bad,* and it had the desired effect. The point is that one generally doesn't have time to figure everything out before speaking, but by knowing and applying the principles of crisis intervention and by reviewing one's work, the proper maneuvers become increasingly spontaneous.

Relabeling is one specific form of plussing. Family members do tend to be labeled, sometimes subtly or even unconsciously, but frequently overtly and blatantly. These labels tend to stick with a person over long periods of time and are usually hard to change. Labels can greatly influence a person's behavior. As a part of his self-image and of the family set, they both reflect and help shape much of the interaction between the person and the family. For example, if Joe is *clumsy,* we will all be watching Joe to see what he might fall over next; we will notice, comment on, and remember every time he falls; and we may not even notice any periods of gracefulness, coordination, or carefulness that he may exhibit. One could imagine that being the constant object of such scrutiny could enhance Joe's tendency toward clumsiness. Sister Janet, in contrast, if subjected to a period of objective scrutiny, might be found to fall over things more frequently than Joe. Her falls may go unnoticed by the family, though, because Janet's label is not *clumsy* but rather *has a good voice*. On those occasions when her falls are noticed, one might hear a comment like "For goodness sakes, Janet, are you trying to act like Joe?"

People tend to behave as they are expected to behave. It is not rare for a young girl's first signs of adolescence—pubertal changes, a slight interest in boys—to be met by her family with reactions of alarm, suspicion, intrusiveness, and restrictiveness. Dire predictions may be issued: "She's boy crazy; she's going to go out with some bum and get herself in trouble." In such cases, she inevitably will.

In a family the labeling may be subtle, but one can often detect the expectations and the accompanying labels by merely listening. Frequently, they will not be subtle: "John is always stealing" (the thief), or "You can't trust her a minute" (the sneak).

In a crisis intervention session, I do not usually comment on these labels, but I try hard to select and use another label, that is, to relabel. Thus, instead of reinforcing the family's label for Mr. Jones—the alcoholic—I will repeatedly and in a variety of ways emphasize what a hard worker he is ("You must be awfully tired after eight hours of that." "And there you were, working your tail off, tired and sweaty, when this phone call from your wife came.").

The "dumb kid" might be relabeled the "baseball player." Early in the first session, I will have learned that he likes baseball. I may emphasize this further by asking who his favorite player is. Later in the session I may use baseball analogies ("I bet when she said that you felt like you'd just struck out."). I may call him "slugger." All of this, of course, may increase his self-esteem and our rapport, but primarily it focuses attention on him in a new way; a different set is established and he is relabeled, at least in the session.

The "nagging wife" might be relabeled the "worried mother"; the "intrusive grandmother" becomes the "lonely widow." Everyone has multiple roles in life, but there is a tendency to focus on only one aspect of a person. We may thus become negative toward a client, for example, not seeing that a woman poorly equipped for mothering may be accomplishing a great deal of good as a community volunteer. This fact doesn't particularly help her kids, but it does describe a part of her. It could be viewed as something that she *is* providing just as easily as it could be viewed as a part of the child-depriving process.

The relabeling process is a plussing maneuver. Thus, it helps establish communication and rapport. Again, although this isn't therapy, the relabeling may plant some seeds that will produce later benefit. At least it conveys the fact that there is more than one way of looking at something, and it introduces some change in perception and roles, part of the system that is often rather rigid. Of course, when a label is recently acquired, as it may be if it is part of the crisis process, this may actually be eliminated by the relabeling. Further, we know that people tend to behave as expected. The new label of a child may exert some influence on this behavior. Thus, when Randy keeps interrupting the conversation, I might comment on how *interested* he is or how *concerned*. I frequently will label a father as *concerned*. Even if he feels quite sure that he is *not* concerned, it may be difficult for him to say that he is not. Being stuck with this label, he may exhibit some motivation or some sense of obligation to live up to it. Few people outrightly reject a positive label, especially if it is applied at the right time and with some shred of evidence to support it.

Finally, the plussing, including the relabeling, seems to have a mysterious power, at least on me. I find that even when I feel I may be going too far or am being too imaginative, even when I am really stretching to dig up something positive about a person or his behavior, I still somehow begin to believe in the positive viewpoint myself. I begin to see the father as really being concerned or to feel the love that lay behind the mother striking her child. The label begins to make sense and to feel right. I do not know whether this means I have conned myself or that I am overcoming my own negative tendencies so that I can perceive positive factors that are actually present. This process may partially fit Murray Bowens' concept of staying detriangled; taking a different stand or a different viewpoint may help me to resist the very powerful pull to get caught up in the family's process, for example, the process of only seeing the father as an alcoholic who causes all of the family's difficulties and dismissing the fact that he's a hard worker. Plussing thus increases my empathy with the client, the rapport becomes stronger from both sides of the relationship, and I become able to deal more effectively with the family.

Paradox

Paradox is a term recently popular in family therapy and used in a variety of ways. Usually, though, it refers to techniques by which clients, especially families, are maneuvered into conflicting positions that force them to change (and, if the therapist sets up the paradox properly, to change for the better). The term is perhaps best associated with the renowned, innovative, and nontraditional therapist Jay Haley. He sees a basic issue of therapy as the struggle for power between therapist and client. I partially subscribe to this view in crisis intervention, as exemplified by my emphasis on taking charge. However, I use the term *paradox* here to refer to a grab bag of maneuvers, each having the feature that its intent is not what it appears to be.

Reversal is very close to Haley's idea of paradox. It consists of arguing against a client's doing what you want him to do. It is most useful when you think he probably won't do what you want anyway. A nice example of this occurred while I was demonstrating the technique of bargaining to a group of mental health workers, using three group members to role play a family. We had worked out an agreement among the family members, and I was ready to have each member sign it. At this point the "mother," beautifully into her role, began to hesitate: "I don't know. You know, somehow it doesn't feel right." Active listening helped to clarify that she agreed with all the terms of the agreement, liked them in fact, but just didn't "feel right signing an agreement with my own child." At this point she had not yet said that she would not sign it but was merely expressing reservations and doubt. I responded as I would have with a real family. I had not yet attempted anything—persuasion, encouragement, or argument—to get her to sign it, and I wasn't about to. At this point I began using reversal:

Therapist: Look, maybe you shouldn't sign it.

Mother: Well, I don't know. You know, it just doesn't feel right.

Therapist: Yeah, I know. Probably you shouldn't sign it. You know, you might sign it and then when you get home you won't feel right and you'll regret it.

Mother: Well, you know, I like the agreements, they really seem pretty good to me.

Therapist: Yeah, I know that, you worked them out where they seemed pretty good, but, you know, with your feelings unsure, you might find it hard to live up to them.

Mother: No, I think I could follow them, that's OK, it's just the idea.

The discussion continued a while longer. Finally I said that I really did not want her to sign the agreement feeling as she did, but we agreed that she could take it home unsigned and think about it, and when the family returned next week we could talk about it.

I have a number of points to make here that would apply to such a situation in real life. The session did *not* end with her defeating me by refusing to sign an agreement that I was trying to push on her. Nor did it end with me set up for later defeat by her signing an agreement that she wasn't going to live up to, and she would've had a ready-made explanation for *not* living up to it—"It just didn't feel right." Instead, the session ended with my refusing, gently but firmly, to let her sign it out of my consideration for her. I *may* allow her to sign it next week. Actually, she could have argued me into letting her sign it—and if that had occurred, I bet she would have stuck to the terms—but she didn't argue hard enough to convince me that she had resolved her conflict, that it felt OK now.

So, either she goes home for a week without signing the agreement and endures the same family hassles and then feels better about signing next week; or the process of working out the agreement may itself lead to some improvements. In the latter case, it may not matter whether she signs the paper or not.

So, I have not asked Mother to do anything that she will refuse to do. She and I have remained on good terms rather than in an adversary position, and I've remained undefeated and therefore "powerful"—I'm very much in charge. The first principle is to stay out of power struggles, and the second is to win if you do get into one.

Another example of reversal that comes up regularly concerns dealing with an uninvolved father. The problem may be to get him to return to the next interview or to get him to do a task before the next session. One point is to choose a task that you think he *will* do. If you can do this, the problem is almost solved before it arises. The principle involved here is twofold; first, ask people to do only what you think they will do, and second, ask them to do what they're going to do anyway. In this instance, I would like Father to return to the next session, but I don't think he will. We've talked enough so that I can anticipate some of his responses if I begin to push by telling him how important it is for him to be here or how essential he is to his son, and so on. These arguments, while valid, are very threatening to the father, suggesting more involvement and responsibility than he wants; they make him feel more inadequate and more guilty ("You haven't been doing enough"), and they endanger his sense of autonomy and manhood if he feels that I'm trying to control him, which I am.

Father: I'm too busy; I have to work; my boss won't let me off.

Therapist: We'll meet in the evening.

Father: I get home too late. I'll be too tired. I don't have
               any ideas anyway; his Mother handles these
               things.

If I push, I'll begin to hear things I really don't want to be said
in the session; even beyond these last few unfortunate statements, by which Father was disqualifying and disengaging
himself, I'll hear "Why should I give up my evenings for him,
he's nothing but a bum anyway. And all this talking is a waste
of time; we've tried all of this before and it doesn't help."

   Now, all of that will very quickly destroy the atmosphere
I've worked hard all session to set. These words have power,
and I don't want them said. So how do I avoid them? What do
I want, and how do I get it? Let us review the situation. I want
Father to return next time, but I don't think he will. I want the
session to end with me in charge and in power, undefeated. I
want to be in a cooperative alliance with Father, and I want
him to still be involved in the process, accepting some responsibility.

   I might proceed by saying, "Now, I think we'll need
another meeting next week to discuss these things further.
Dad, look, I know how concerned you are and how much you
want to help. But look, you're working hard, you might have
trouble getting more time off from the boss, or if we meet in
the evening you'll be pretty tired out. Don't you think it's
putting a little too much on you for you to try to attend?"

   Now, I have given Father the option of arguing with me
and persuading me to let him attend. If I've done a good job
of anticipating his arguments and saying them first, I really
haven't left him much to say, unless he wants to argue that he
should come. His two options are to join in an agreement with
me or to come, so either way I "win." A devious-minded
person may even suspect that the above statements present a
certain challenge to Father's manhood or even an invitation to
wonder why he isn't wanted at the next session and what's
going to be done behind his back. Father might respond to a
challenge or with a suspicion if he's so inclined.

In the above statement to Father, I left things open. He can choose whether to attend, we can discuss it, and I'll get a better idea of how he feels and how he is responding to the whole intervention. Sometimes I will push a little harder initially. In this case, I can still do so:

"Look, you've probably even been wondering if this will do any good; I mean you've tried things that didn't work before, and it would really be overloading you to ask you to take more of your time to come in, especially when you feel it's a long shot."

"Look, I know how concerned you are, but there's a limit to what one man can do; you're working hard, and you've tried. Wouldn't it be better if you don't try to come in next time?"

In this last statement, I've pushed it to an extreme. I've read that Father almost certainly is *not* going to be willing to come in, no matter what I do; therefore, I'm *asking* him to do what I'm sure he's going to do anyway.

In this discussion of reversal, I have alluded to two of the issues underlying paradox. The first is a question of power. I want to stay in a position of power with the clients. To do so, I need to stay undefeated. However, in reality I have little or no power. Therefore, I am very cautious about what I ask people to do. I'll make only those requests to which I'll get a yes. I'll maneuver so that what they're doing appears to be at my request, in cooperation with me.

This first issue of power fades right into the second issue of alliance. At all times I try to maintain or work toward a state of alliance with the clients—we are on the same team—and to avoid an adversary position. I wish to avoid threatening them, because a threat causes a defensive response and a diminished alliance, if I seem more enemy than friend. I particularly wish to avoid a real, nonparadoxical argument. Argument means that the client is spending his mental energy to defend his position against me. Many people find it hard to give up a position once taken—it becomes a matter of self-esteem, honor, and saving face. Whenever someone exhibits a defense, there is some reason for it, and the defense will probably not be easily overcome. Thus, if I anticipate disagreement, I try to avoid pushing someone to the point where he will even take a position on a subject. I try to fish for hints, to feel him out first. If on occasion he does disagree, does take a position, I try not to push further. I try to avoid mobilization of his defenses, which makes him more rigidly in disagreement. If I can drop it, shift away from disagreement before his defenses are up, he may later be able to consider what I've said about the issue and even be able to shift his position.

Thus, I will raise a point, and if the client disagrees, I will drop it and move on. I will use a disclaimer, as in the earlier example ("Sometimes I get these weird psychiatry ideas, but . . . ."). This means he can listen to the idea without feeling threatened—it is already "defanged" for him, and he can see I'm not going to push it. I am not setting up a direct confrontation of my idea against his. It can also be seen how active listening helps avoid conflict; the therapist remains in a very noncommittal position, neither agreeing nor disagreeing, and it remains clear that he has not done so ("I see, Mr. Jones, you feel that . . . ." or "It is your idea that . . . .").

This issue of alliance fades into a third issue, the magic of words. This is a rather shaky idea in some ways, but I think it has some validity. The idea is simply that words do have power, and that the mere saying of an idea may accomplish something. For example, in the discussion of labeling, I emphasized how much power a label can carry and the importance of relabeling. In crisis intervention I will try to just get certain ideas *said,* and said in such a way that they are not too threatening and do not lead to defensiveness or a direct conflict or confrontation with someone. There are two ideas involved; first, if defenses are not raised against an idea, it can sink into the unconscious (or maybe even remain in consciousness) and influence things, maybe leading to eventual change. Maybe later it can reemerge into consciousness, where it can be actively used. I call this planting a seed. Second, if I can smuggle an idea into the session without its being denied, maybe I can bring it up later as though we've already agreed to it. At least I've given it a trial run and seen if anyone jumped too high, so I can better decide if it's safe to bring it up or not.

The next two paradoxical maneuvers, speaking past the point and speaking to the wrong person, directly apply to this last idea of getting the "magic words" said safely. That is, these are ways to say something without inciting defensiveness, which will leave the ideas negated, without disrupting the alliance, and without losing power.

Speaking past the point is almost self-explanatory. You can say all kinds of things if you don't let them develop into a confrontation. One way is to say something and then keep talking, finally focusing on some other issue ("I'm sure you'll like my book, I'll put you down to order two copies. Do you think these orange covers are good or would another color have been better?" "Mr. Jones, you've just heard your wife's concerns about your drinking, and I expect you've worried about it yourself from time to time, but do you think there are other areas in your marriage that could maybe become more satisfying for the two of you?").

Speaking to the wrong person is a particularly effective maneuver. I can say all kinds of things about Mr. Jones as long as I don't say them *to* him—then he won't feel honor bound to argue:

"So, Mrs. Jones, you're concerned about your husband's drinking, and although he'd probably deny it, of course, haven't you ever thought he's probably concerned about it sometimes too? Do you notice that sometimes men feel they have to maintain an iron man image and deny any problems for fear they'll look weak, or maybe so it won't look like the wife is calling the shots?"

"Well, Mrs. Jones, you're upset because Tommy rejects the idea of going to counseling. Now he may have some good reasons. You know that sometimes kids get the idea that getting help means you're weak, or they may even think it means you're crazy. Of course, you realize that lots of people find it helpful to talk things over with a professional, knowing that it'll be kept completely private and that they won't be pushed into anything. But it certainly takes courage to start.

Who knows, someday Tommy might decide it's a good idea, but it sure doesn't sound like he's ready right now, does it?"

"Yes, and" is a very simple technique for getting things said without argument and disagreement. Since the magic of words can apply adversely, it is sometimes important not to leave harmful statements standing uncountered. This technique is particularly effective in such countering. The simple principle is that if you disagree with someone and say "No" or "I disagree," they will be inclined to argue. This can be easily avoided.

Patient:	Doctor, all psychiatrists are quacks who are only out to soak their patients.
Therapist:	[*a psychiatrist*] Yes, and have you been aware of how helpful they are and that they're usually very concerned about their patients' welfare?

Patient:	Doctor, this boy here is the worst son I've had. All boys are bad, though, and will get away with whatever they can.
Therapist:	Yes, although sometimes they're honest and thoughtful, the very same kids can be pretty rotten sometimes.

Frequently the client will agree with the "yes, and" statement or at least not debate it. This technique can also be combined with talking past the point to further diminish argument.

Being wrong is an effective maneuver, particularly when people aren't very responsive or spontaneous in discussion. It obtains an answer for information value and at the same time allows you to interject some ideas you wish to introduce without debate.

Worker:	What'd your father do then, John?
John:	Nuthin' much.
Worker:	He probably hit you alongside the head with a two by four, right?

John: Naw, he just slapped me around a little.

Worker: So I guess at that point Mary said something to you like "Look, Mom, as much as I appreciate your concern, you're really butting into my business, and I'd rather make my own mistakes"?

Mother: No, Mary wouldn't talk to me like that.

Worker: Oh, she wasn't that polite about it, huh?

Mother: Oh, no, she just said, "OK, Ma, if you say so."

This latter example would also illustrate speaking to the wrong person and using the magic of words since Mary is also in the room.

A somewhat similar process to being wrong is to be ignorant or uninformed. If I can develop a set in the session where the process consists of the family members collaborating to explain things to me—they're the teachers and I'm the student—this seems a particularly efficacious situation. This might start with the father explaining to me the technical details of his job and then evolve through the family explaining what happened Saturday night and then how the family functions ("Oh, I see now, it's like responsibilities. You mean like Mom usually takes care of things with the kids and Dad pays the bills?").

Perhaps paradoxically, this type of process doesn't interfere with my being in charge or maintaining power, but it reduces a lot of the struggles about it. I believe being wrong or being ignorant produces in the client an automatic urge to correct and reduces his feeling of being threatened by a supersmart therapist who can see through him and tell all his secrets. It increases the client's self-esteem by putting him in a more prestigious position.

"You don't mean" is a maneuver related to plussing. It can be useful in the session when someone is acting in a destructive way; for example, if Mother is provoking a lot of guilt, or subtly name calling, or attacking ("[To Mother] You certainly don't mean to make Johnny feel guilty; you're trying to clarify how much he means to you?" "I know you're not trying to make Johnny feel bad. Are you trying to show what a

wrong impression someone might get of him from some of his behavior?").

I don't really understand why, but such comments tend to bring the undesired behavior to a halt. I've certainly had more success with this method than with direct confrontation:

Worker: You're trying to make him feel guilty.

Mother: You're damn right I am, the little bastard ought to feel guilty. Wouldn't you feel guilty if you treated your Mother this way?

Requesting the symptom, one of Haley's major ideas, is to ask someone to do what they're already doing but to request it in a way that makes the action more noxious to them, or gives the therapist more control over the action, or both. It is a technique I rarely use in the same way that Haley does because it generally doesn't work for me. In Haley's approach, when the patient returns for the next session he has generally not cooperated with the therapeutic request, so as a result, the symptom is diminished. The therapist must then chastise him for the lack of cooperation. I have never been able to this with a straight face. The whole thing doesn't feel right to me.

Nonetheless, I do request the symptom occasionally during a session to deal with a particular piece of disruptive or destructive behavior. For example, suppose Mr. Jones constantly interrupts his wife and I haven't been able to stop it. Also, assume that I've sensed that my directly *asking* him to stop it will probably not be effective. In this case, I might say, "Mr. Jones, can we try a little experiment? This may not make good sense, but I want to try something and see how it goes, OK? For the next five minutes, I'll time it, would you interrupt your wife everytime she starts to say something?"

Mr. Jones may or may not do it, even after he agrees to. If he doesn't, I'll push him. After the five minutes, I'll do something to wind the experiment up—ask how each of them felt, or whatever—and then go on with the session. Usually Mr. Jones's interruptions will be less frequent. I presume this is because he has become more aware of his behavior in a way that didn't challenge him to continue it in order to beat me, and also because now his interrupting has seemed to come somewhat at my behest, under my control; thus, to preserve autonomy, he doesn't do it anymore.

Exaggeration is a maneuver I rarely use, because I feel certain dangers are involved. I have used it on a few occasions, and so far it has worked. One type of occasion is when parents have brought their child to me, with a primary purpose of proving how totally incorrigible the child is. If all my efforts have failed to change either this set or the subject in any appreciable way, then—and only then—do I try exaggeration, which consists of listening to the parents and beginning to respond with comments like the following:

"Is that so?"

"He did?!?"

"You must've been near the end of your rope!"

"You must've felt like killing him."

"That's horrible! And this has been going on six months?"

"My God! I don't see how you've stood six months of this. You must be about to collapse."

"This has been driving you both crazy. It's a miracle you've stood it this long. What in the world happened next?"

If this maneuver works, and so far it always has, I eventually hear a shift from "Yeah, and let me tell you what he did next" to "Well, Doc, it hasn't been quite *that* bad," "Well, Doc, you know he hasn't been doing this all the time," or "Sure, Doc, but you know he's got some good qualities, too."

When these shifts occur, I somewhat dubiously and cautiously let them persuade me a bit and then shift the subject to something else altogether. Notice that in these comments, I never directly attacked the child, only the situation, although I think in practice I have at times said something almost about the kid ("My God, he sounds like a monster!"). I have not yet had a kid take offense at this maneuver—I'm not sure why. What I have observed is that once I begin joining the parents in attacking their kid, the parents eventually start defending him.

I do wish to emphasize that I have only used this maneuver a few times, and although it has worked so far, I'm afraid of it. I fear that if it doesn't work, if the shift doesn't occur, it might be quite destructive. Therefore, I only use it as a last resort, when I feel the situation is being lost anyway.

Chapter Five

Assessing Problems, Resources, and Strengths

All of the steps of crisis intervention except the final one are conducted simultaneously and continuously until near the end of the intervention. As the work progresses, the emphasis shifts from establishing communication and rapport (Step 1), to assessing the problem (Step 2), to assessing resources and strengths (Step 3), and beyond.

Thus, assessing the problem begins with the first contact about the case, usually the first phone call from the client. At the outset, however, the worker must devote most of his attention and activity toward establishing communication and rapport, as described in Step 1. Thereafter, continuing attention and effort must be directed to *maintenance*, that is, to maintaining what has been established. Each step or phase of the intervention process presents its own special problems of maintenance.

As the goals of Step 1 are accomplished, more of the worker's attention is shifted to assessing the problem. The worker must develop a formulation that includes three components. First, he must quickly obtain some grasp of the family's immediate situation. This includes some idea of their perception of the situation and some idea of the family system. Second, he must develop a formulation of the crisis process, the chain of events that led up to the crisis. Third, he must define The Problem that initiated the chain of events. In a similar fashion, resources and strengths are looked for and noted from the very beginning of the intervention, with increasing emphasis on this step as the work progresses, particularly as The Problem begins to reach formulation.

From the first contact, it is worthwhile to use whatever information is available, whether from a folder, a referring colleague, or the family's phone call. For instance, the worker can note who makes the first call, how that person defines the problem, his general approach and attitude, and so on. Does Mother do the calling or does Father handle contacts outside the family? Is Mother calling because she's concerned and upset, or is she calling for Father or because the school said she should? The worker can ask a few pertinent questions, being careful not to get too involved in the call or to obtain too much information, as discussed previously.

The worker begins to use information obtained from this initial conversation. He must quickly decide if crisis intervention is indicated, how urgent the situation is, and who should come to the first session. He must decide how to present all of this to the client. I have no set pattern in this, but I generally prefer to get everyone possible to come to the first session, and I do this as much as I can without getting into a power struggle. I will take what I can get, however, and work with whomever attends. From the clues available, the worker must hypothesize the nature of the situation and of the family system and formulate tentative plans for the entire intervention, but especially for the first session. These plans include consideration of various types of maneuvers he might use and of various goals and subgoals he might set. Obviously all of these plans are tentative, and the worker must be prepared to quickly alter all or any number of his ideas as necessary. Nonetheless, this early work provides a framework for establishing an organized approach and helps the worker to stay oriented and avoid being swamped by a mass of unorganized data. This is like a chess game, in which one makes moves according to an overall plan of attack. As the session unfolds, one may have to change plans extensively and repeatedly, but it is foolish to begin play without any definite purpose in mind.

While conducting the meeting phase of the first session, the worker further notes various clues about the family system: Who sits where, who takes charge, what are the moods and the communication styles? Do the parents seat themselves on opposite sides of the room or together? Does someone try to speak for the kids, or does someone tell them which chairs to take? Does someone try to take over the session? These clues should be used to get a quick grasp of the family system and its functioning—alliances, rules, strengths, and so on.

An in-depth analysis of the family system is more properly the province of family therapy than of crisis intervention. Here only the more obvious rudiments are essential or entirely relevant. A quick analysis of the family system will make it easier to handle the session by going along with the system wherever possible, dealing more directly with certain aspects of it where necessary, anticipating problems, staying in charge, and making plans that are not only reasonable but also are likely to work. These clues and these ideas about the family system also help shape the worker's hypotheses about the crisis situation and the problems. Of course, as the work proceeds, the worker continually learns more about the family, and all of these formulations are altered and expanded.

These assessments, formulations, and plans are made by the worker as the session gets under way. At the same time, his mind is on the work of Step 1, establishing communication and rapport, and he can utilize some of the ideas for guidance in that process. Meanwhile, in the actual overt interaction of the session, the worker first meets the family members and then moves into the open, formal portion of problem assessment. The session, particularly the assessing, must "begin where they are," that is, with the family's problem and complaints as they see them. Thus, I extend the introductions and the meeting phase so that a bit of time can be spent on building a relationship and making the family more comfortable, but then I ask about the problem. I have no special or favorite way of doing so; it depends on the interactions and the formulations up to that point, but of course I do note the manner in which the family responds—who speaks and how, and so on.

As the family begins to express their ideas, active listening is most useful initially to increase rapport and communication and to gather information. However, in pursuing Step 1, a number of other moves will also be indicated. Thus, while actively listening, the worker will also be plussing, taking charge, getting details, focusing on facts, reducing anxiety, relabeling, and emphasizing certain bits of information.

I will stick primarily with active listening as long as the story is unfolding in a useful fashion and with the desired atmosphere. If things are going especially well, I may become more questioning and let the family "teach" me by explaining things. Active listening may be resumed whenever needed, especially to deal with feelings and resistances that may arise during the process.

During the initial stage of assessment, the focus is on the current situation, the here-and-now. Not all families begin at that point but most do, and it should be gently encouraged, since it makes the assessment easier and more orderly. While learning about the current situation, the worker should be asking himself certain questions. Using the definition given earlier, he should reassess: Is this a crisis? If so, for whom? Is crisis intervention advisable? A second set of questions addresses the system and resources: Who is in the most distress? Who seems motivated for the work? Who seems calm, who verbal, who intelligent? Where are the alliances and the strains within the system? Who seems ready to work with me and who opposed? Where are the most likely obstacles to the work? The third set of questions the worker asks himself and may occasionally ask the family. This set addresses the relationship of the clients to the intervention: Why did they come here? What do they want and expect? Why did they come *now,* why not last week or next week?

Once the worker can answer these questions for himself, he is in a much better position. These questions are not usually directly asked of the family, since they may lead to premature closure; that is, in answering the questions, the family will take a position in regard to the situation, the work, and the worker, and things may gel into an undesirable set. Of course, the family already has their set before they come in, but as long as it is not openly voiced, they can be more flexible—things are more negotiable and open to change without their losing face or developing a power struggle with the worker. Thus, while the worker is addressing these questions in his own mind, he may need to divert the family from them, at least for a while.

This problem will be clarified using as an example one of the two major special maintenance problems of the Step 2 phase, the issue of what the clients want. It is usually better, at least at first, not to pose this issue for the clients directly. They frequently have their hidden agenda, and it may be best to leave it hidden for the time being. Otherwise, there may be a premature, disruptive, and frequently nasty confrontation as the clients openly push for and demand what they want. This occurs because the clients feel desperate and helpless. They have tried solutions and failed. They finally have either passively decided that the only possible solution is for the worker to take care of them altogether or actively decided that the only possible salvation is for the worker to provide some one thing that they genuinely believe is the unique, crucial, and magical key to all their problems.

Because they are in crisis, often what the family wants reflects their wish for immediate symptom relief, to escape the pain rather than to solve the problem. Once what they want is out in the open, the clients tend to become more desperate and feel driven to find out if they can get what they want, especially as it becomes increasingly clear that the worker cannot or will not provide it. Frequently, the family wants their problems magically solved without needing to do anything. Sometimes they want their spouse changed, their child put away, or special exemption from agency rules. Sometimes this demand stemming from desperation must be carefully differentiated from attempts at simple manipulation, depending on what the family problem is. I know of no simple way to do this other than to draw on intuition, experience, careful history taking, and ultimately clinical judgment. Occasionally what the client wants turns out to be both appropriate and available. Most crisis situations are not that easy.

At the beginning the worker needs time; to establish a relationship with the family that the family will value, to instill the family with hope and some sense of adequacy and competence, to help the family change some of their perceptions of the situation, and to begin working out with the family some of the alternatives that can be pursued. Hopefully, the worker will have time for these things before being confronted with what the family wants, and especially before the clients must face the fact that they are not going to get what they want. They must have something to hang on to before being deprived of what *they* initially see as their only hope. If the worker can develop the session successfully, the question of what the family wants may never come up at all. Or the question may only have to be looked at as one of several alternatives, and the clients may be able to decide that it is not the most desirable alternative. At worst, they may eventually be able to accept that it is not really a viable alternative at all. Thus, not letting the question of what the family wants arise prematurely is an important part of maintenance.

Once the present situation is discussed and assessed, with communication and rapport not only maintained but also further established, it is time to lead the discussion into the recent past. The goal is to unravel and outline a chain of events—of stresses, reactions, and problem-solving efforts. To accomplish this requires a complex shifting of focus from present to past and back again. This continuing process of Step 2 is interwoven with maneuvers designed to emphasize certain points, to integrate the data into a logical and coherent sequence, and to maintain communication and rapport. The primary emphasis is reality and behaviorally oriented—upon events and situations and upon reactions to them. Feelings and motives are not emphasized except as needed for an empathic response, necessary ventilation, or plussing:

"Well, when did you *first* feel things weren't going well?"

"You must've been awfully upset. How had things been going just before that?"

"What did you do next?"

"Now, that had happened just before you blew up at her?" Finally things can be pulled together:

"Now let me see if I understand. You left Jane and the kids shortly after your mother died. Before she died, you could always count on your mother if things were going bad. And *just before* she died, you were worrying about what the doctor might say about Jane's Pap test? And Jane, you'd been worried about that for a while, too? That's when you were having the insomnia? And Frank, even with all of this kind of piling up at once, nothing had blown up yet, everything was moving along fairly well, up until the time the boss said you might be getting laid off?"

The worker tries—with as much collaboration and involvement from the clients as he can get—to outline a chain of events, emphasizing the relationship of each event to the ones preceding and following, in such a way that the sequence is logical and makes sense both to the worker and to the clients. This will greatly enhance everyone's understanding of the crisis situation, and it will suggest areas and types of interventions to try. Equally or more important is the value of this process to the family, since it illustrates to them that their various behaviors have been understandable responses to their situations, rather than being totally incomprehensible or malevolent. They can see their current situation as the logical outcome of a comprehensible process, and so it seems less unfathomable, unmanageable, and overwhelming. This decreases blaming and feelings of helplessness and guilt, and it enhances thinking, fact gathering, and problem solving.

While establishing the chain of events, the worker must

seek additional information. He must learn more about how the family operates. He wants to know what coping maneuvers the family has already tried, how they worked, and why they didn't. He doesn't want to come up with an elaborate plan and find out "We've already tried that!" Such a deflating faux pas markedly reduces his credibility and his power. Reviewing the family's failed efforts enhances their tendency to listen to the worker's ideas. He might also wish to ask about previous crises—how they were dealt with and why those techniques didn't work this time. This review of previously surmounted difficulties helps improve the clients' self-image and increases hope.

During all this data gathering, assessing, and formulating, the worker should be mentally filling in Aquilera and Messick's lists, noting the inadequacies in perception, network, and coping mechanisms that caused the present situation to become a crisis. It may be easier to do this on paper during the discussion. This formulation helps to organize the information and will quickly suggest intervention strategies. At this point, The Problem has not yet been defined, and the final entries cannot be made into the lists, but the possibilities can be noted. As these possible entries are heard, they should be underlined with the clients ("Your mother, who you'd always been able to depend on, had just died, so of course these other problems were really coming up at a bad time for you, weren't they?"). Thus, constructing the chain of events and filling in Aquilera and Messick's lists merge together.

The series of links that is developed eventually forms a chain that leads back to the unresolved problem responsible for the crisis process. Thus, the chain of events connects the present crisis situation logically with The Problem. In the usual course of events, The Problem is determined and defined last. Usually in the search for The Problem, many possibilities arise, and there is a certain latitude in selecting one. Once one is selected, there are always many words to choose from to express it.

Problems could be loosely divided into two groups, catastrophic and developmental. Most situations show elements of both. *Catastrophic* refers to a specific event, usually abrupt and unexpected—a death or losing a job. Developmental problems, which usually are more difficult to define and to treat, arise out of gradual processes, often of a relatively normal nature—an adolescent's growing rebelliousness, a younger child's becoming more autonomous, or Father's increasing alcoholism. Obviously, mixtures of the two types of problems arise frequently—Father's increasing drinking finally costs him his job. If the chain of events has been well developed, we might choose to define The Problem as Father's losing his job, his inability to find a new one, his increasing drinking, the family's inability to cope with Father's job loss or his increased drinking, or Father's difficulty adjusting to the death of his mother (which seems to have played a part in his increased drinking). The chain of events could be traced back to any of these problems, although sometimes the nature and timing of the turmoil may focus more attention on one of them. In this example, I would not suggest defining The Problem as "Father's drinking."

This example illustrates several important points. First, although a crisis is time limited and will end within six weeks, the problem that initiated the crisis may have developed at some earlier point. Often, however, The Problem selected is one that developed relatively close to the onset of the crisis, and it is usually easier to work with in this latter case, because it usually makes more sense to the family and keeps the situation simple. In our example, Father has been drinking heavily for many years. While his drinking has certainly played its part in some family difficulties, it has been coped with without causing a crisis. For these reasons we wouldn't define Father's drinking as The Problem.

Second, if The Problem is defined as Father's drinking, Mother will probably enthusiastically agree, delivering a long lecture about how she has been delivering long lectures about this for years. She will be most impressed and pleased at seeing how wise and perceptive the worker is. Father, however, may be somewhat less enthused. He may become tearful and agree that it's all his fault; he may swear never to touch another drop; he may become rather silent and withdrawn; or, most likely, he will explain that he doesn't drink all that much and that he can stop any time he wants to. It's hard to predict exactly how he'll react in this session, but it's not hard to predict that he won't react at all in the next session—he won't be there. The point is that the definition of The Problem must be *palatable*—that is, it must not overly offend, attack, or threaten any of the clients. Also, it should make some sense to the clients in terms of their experiences and their ways of looking at things. One doesn't usually suggest to an Italian family that the problem is living too close to Grandfather, or to a West Virginia farmer that his wife needs him to talk to her more or to help her with the housework.

Third, if The Problem is defined as Father's drinking, we are stuck with the prospect of trying to do something about it. My record in getting people to stop drinking is not very good, and I am plussing when I say that. We can save ourselves a lot of frustration by trying to define a problem that we can do something about. This I call defining The Problem in *workable* terms. One issue is which problem to select, and another is in choosing the words to define it. For example, I would never define a problem as "Mother died," about which nothing can be done, or even as "the family can't adjust to Mother's death." Rather, thinking in terms of hope and expectations, plussing, labeling, and the magic of words, I would choose to say, "The family has not yet adjusted to Mother's death."

So, in defining The Problem, one has wide latitude in choosing and expressing it, and these choices should be thoughtfully and carefully exercised. The definition chosen should have some accuracy and make sense to the clients, it should be palatable, and it should be workable.

A detailed exploration is done in Step 2. Once the chain of events, Aquilera and Messick's lists, and The Problem have been worked out, we have a formulation of the entire crisis process as the family has lived it. The worker may wish to summarize the formulation with the clients. Or, the formulation may have been developed clearly enough and with enough family involvement that a summary is not needed. Or, some aspects of the formulation may be too unpalatable to be shared and can best be left implied. As a matter of fact, I rarely describe The Problem to the family in explicit terms but merely talk about what has happened: "And since then, you haven't adjusted to it yet." It is most important that the family be actively involved in the process of working out the formulation, and that it be developed in such a way that they agree with it at the end. Of course, again, this is not accomplished by telling them, "We're all going to work out a formulation" or by formally asking them if they agree with it (thereby giving them a big opening to *disagree*), but rather by doing it through each link of the chain and each step of the process ("So, Mr. Jones, if I understand it, when your Mother died, of course you were pretty upset, right? And then . . . , is that about right?").

This introduces the second special aspect of maintenance, which is specific to Step 2: the question of what should be dealt with openly and what should remain unshared, kept within the worker's mind. As much should be shared with the family and worked out with their collaboration as they can handle. However, there are times when The Problem seems so clear that there is not much latitude available, and even with the most carefully chosen words it would remain unpalatable to the family. Then I will not define that problem. I may choose another problem entirely or a closely related problem, or just not define any problem at all. I may choose to imply the problem, to discuss it through innuendo or in metaphor, or to avoid it completely except in my own mind. It is essential to keep guessing what the clients can accept, comprehend, and work with, and what may be too threatening, abstract, or foreign to their way of thinking. For guidance, I use trial balloons, watching their reactions to related topics, to innuendos, and to mild comments before deciding to go further into a subject.

While pursuing the assessing work of Steps 2 and 3, the worker is also engaged in work on Steps 4 and 5, planning and mobilizing. Through the assessment process itself, a plan of action should begin to suggest itself, and this plan is one of the goals of assessment. In formulating a plan, the worker will want to capitalize on the family's strengths and incorporate them into the plan. While the family may learn and grow during the intervention process, a crisis is not the time to try to institute a number of totally new skills and behaviors. The more the capabilities of the family are used, the more their self-esteem will be enhanced, the less additional stress they'll be placed under, and, most important, the more likely they will be to follow the plan. This is an important aspect of mobilizing the family.

The training of most workers in the mental health field has had a pathology orientation. It seems easier to detect someone's problems or flaws than their strengths and assets. It may take a definite effort to see positive features, but it is important for crisis intervention work. The worker will need to look for problems and defects in the situation and in the system, while trying to focus on the strengths of the individuals. Once this shift in thinking is made, the process of assessing strengths and resources is simple and straightforward. While considering the inadequacies to fill in Aquilera and Messick's lists, one might also consider the adequate factors, especially coping mechanisms and network.

While tracing the crisis background with the clients, the worker might also ask about previous problems or crises and how they were resolved. This helps clarify what went wrong this time, improves the self-image and increases hope, and also reveals some of the useful skills, techniques, and coping mechanisms already available in the family's repertoire. These might then be used in a way that the family has not considered, or perhaps their use was blocked by an obstacle that might be overcome. For example, if Mother were not so embarrassed about what's happened, she might call Grandma, who would help as she always has before.

It is important that the worker be familiar with community resources, but of particular importance are the family's own resources that are already in their support network. These include relatives, friends, neighbors, coworkers, churches, other organizations, and community agencies. The presence of these resources may usually be detected by asking about them at various relevant points in the discussion rather than obviously going after "who could help." Thus, if Mother mentions someone in her extended family, the worker might ask about her other family members and then naturally inquire where Father's family lives. In the meeting phase, I frequently ask about jobs and hobbies and what the people like to do in their spare time, and then I might in passing wonder if Mother attends church, which usually elicits the whole family's relationship to church. In this way I also begin to learn about talents and skills that hopefully can be utilized, both in relabeling and as a resource. During the interview I listen for additional such resources, and I also look for the presence of other individual assets, such as intelligence, gregariousness, practical mindedness, and so on.

Having determined individual resources, the worker must determine their availability. Is the person with me or against me? Involved in the intervention process or withdrawn? In a position of influence in the family or ostracized? Caught up in the crisis process or functioning fairly well? These factors can be crucial when trying to incorporate existing resources into the plan of action.

Role playing is a technique that is probably familiar to many readers. I don't use it very often in crisis intervention, but it is sometimes quite valuable in the assessment phase when the interview is foundering. A family may be too angry and emotions out of hand. Or the opposite may be true—the family may be withdrawn, guarded, lifeless, and uncommunicative. I also use role playing when a family stays very vague and unfocused. Depending on the family and the mood of the session, I'll either slide into role playing unobtrusively or stop and formally ask for everyone's permission to try something and then just start.

Mother: He's always coming in late.

Interviewer: What time does he come in?

Mother:	Late, always late.
Interviewer:	Well, what time usually? 10:00 P.M.? Midnight?
Mother:	Whatever time, any time, he never listens, he doesn't care, he's no good.
Interviewer:	Johnny, what time do you usually come in?
Johnny:	I don't know.
Interviewer:	Pop, what time does he usually come in?
Pop:	I don't know. Like she said, he doesn't listen.
Interviewer:	What do you do when he comes in late?
Mother:	What can I do? Have you ever seen a child that wouldn't listen to his mother? And the disrespect! It's driving me crazy!
Interviewer:	Johnny, what does your mother do when you come in late?
Johnny:	I don't know.
Interviewer:	Mom, where are you usually when Johnny comes in late? Are you asleep, or in the kitchen, or where?
Mother:	Asleep? How can I sleep? I worry and worry and worry.
Interviewer:	So, where were you last time? You sit up and worry, right?
Mother:	Right, I worry.
Interviewer:	And last time you were sitting in the kitchen, worrying, when he came in, right?
Mother:	No, I sat in the living room. I can't sleep.
Interviewer:	And you're in the living room. And he comes in—the front door? [Mother nods.] And who spoke? Did he say something? "Hello, Mom?" Or did you say something?
Mother:	Him, speak? You'd think he'd speak to his own mother?
Interviewer:	So you spoke first. What did you say to him?

Mother:	What can I say? He never listens.
Interviewer:	So, what *did* you say, to a boy who never listens? You must've said, "Gee, son, I'm glad you're home, I've got some nice, warm soup on the stove."
Mother:	Soup? Hah! He don't want soup, he just wants that pot, dope, more pot.
Interviewer:	So what'd you say?
Mother:	I told him any kind of a son . . . .
Interviewer:	No, tell him.
Mother:	Huh?
Interviewer:	Tell him, now, like you did.
Mother:	Well, I told him . . . .
Interviewer:	No, no, say it to him.
Mother:	To him?
Interviewer:	Yeah, right, say it to him.
Mother:	Well, I told you . . . .
Interviewer:	No, excuse me, no, say it like you said it then. Say, like, "Johnny, I've told you and told you to come in, and . . . ."
Mother:	Oh, like I said it, "OK, Johnny, why are you late again?"
Interviewer:	Johnny, what do you say?
Johnny:	I don't know.
Interviewer:	So, Mother said, "Why are you late?" and Johnny said, "I don't know."
Mother:	No, he didn't say that.
Interviewer:	Well, what did he say?
Mother:	I don't know, I can't remember.
Interviewer:	Well, you said, "Johnny, why are you late again?" and he probably said, "Gee, Mom, I'm awfully sorry, you know it breaks my heart to see you so

upset like this," and he probably had tears in his eyes. Right, Johnny?

Johnny: Naw.

Interviewer: Huh?

Johnny: Naw. I didn't say that.

Interviewer: Oh, you probably said, "To be honest, Mom, I was trying to hold up three gas stations in one night, and there was a cop at the last one, so it took longer."

Johnny: Naw.

Interviewer: Huh?

Johnny: Naw, I said, "Get off my back."

Interviewer: Say it to her, now.

Johnny: Huh?

Interviewer: Say it to her. [If Johnny won't, the interviewer would play his role.]

Johnny: Get off my back.

Interviewer: And what did you say, Mom?

Mother: Well, I told him . . . .

Interviewer: No, tell him now.

Mother: Oh. I said, "Well, who wouldn't . . . ."

Interviewer: No, just say it to him like you said it.

Mother: Oh, OK. Who wouldn't be on your back with you doping all the time and I can't sleep for worry?

Interviewer: Johnny, answer her.

Johnny: Yeah, well, you're on my back all the time. Anyway, I can take care of myself.

Interviewer: OK. Pop, where were you?

Pop: Huh?

Interviewer: Where were you during this conversation? You were alseep, you were in the living room, what?

Pop: Oh, yeah, I was in the kitchen.

Interviewer:	OK, you're in the kitchen. Here, sit over here, this is the kitchen now, OK? Now, what're you doing? Having a coffee, having a beer, fixing a sandwich, what?
Pop:	A coffee.
Interviewer:	OK, you're in the kitchen, having a coffee, and you hear this. What do you do? [Interviewer sets the stage, shifting to present tense.]
Pop:	I go in there.
Interviewer:	OK, come in here now, from the kitchen, leave your coffee, right?, and come in. Now say what you said then.
Pop:	I said to Johnny . . . .
Interviewer:	No, say to him now.
Pop:	Oh, OK. Johnny, you know that's no way to speak to your mother.
Johnny:	Yeah, well, I'll speak to her any way I want. How come you never say nothing about the way she speaks to me, didn't you hear that?

Now that they're rolling, I'll let them go a bit, prodding or clarifying where I need to. When somebody starts getting too hot, I'll interrupt with some questions. As they begin to get into the swing of this, they'll begin to sense that they are exposing themselves and some of the actual workings of the family. They'll balk, and I'll have to hold them to it.

| *Mother:* | Well, this isn't the way it usually goes, it can be different sometimes. |
| *Interviewer:* | Well, good, OK, I'm interested in how it usually goes, but we're in this one right now, OK? So, what do you say to Johnny now? |

As we follow this out, what I'll eventually learn is that Mother keeps Father awake with her half the night, and he's groggy the next day at work. He's also about ready to kill her and could personally care less what time Johnny comes in or if he comes in at all. I also learn that Mother, who is in crisis, sleeps half the next day and has become something of a recluse. By the end of the session, Johnny will have agreed as a sacrifice for Mother's welfare to call her between 11 and 12 o'clock any night he's out (which he may or may not do). Mother has reluctantly agreed that while that isn't what she wants, at least it's better than what she's been getting. She has also agreed to call the community hotline anytime she's worried or upset about Johnny and to have her Aunt Emma, who has raised three boys with moderate success, over for lunch within two days to discuss things. Pop has agreed that his behavior has been totally irresponsible, jeopardizing his family's security by ruining his health because he lets Mother keep him up at night. He has agreed to refuse to come downstairs with her at night anymore. These agreements, which will be only partially observed, have reduced tension and bought some time, shifted the focus and perception of the family, and hopefully will obtain some support for Mother while reducing Pop's general animosity. The family has some sense of hope, is moving, and is thinking more in a problem-solving style.

During this example, I mentioned some of the gimmicks I use with this role-playing technique. I set the scene, sometimes using props. I'm deliberately wrong in order to provoke a correction. I use various interruptions to facilitate and maintain the role-playing process, to maintain my control of the session, to regulate the level of emotionality, and to slow the process so that the family members can take a look at what's unfolding. A frequent interruption is the checks "Now, does that sound about right?" and "Is that about the way it was?" The interruptions keep the family involved in the process without getting carried away, and they keep them involved with *me* in the process. They keep the task of communicating in focus and save me from going through a long role play only to hear "Actually, that isn't anything like what happens at home."

If a family member is absent or won't participate, I then

have an opportunity to play the role, which allows me to make all kinds of statements that I could never otherwise get away with.

Interviewer: Let's see, now, I'm being Johnny. What would Johnny say? How about this. "OK, Mom, I know you're right, and I know I'm ruining my life, but can't you see I just don't have enough self-confidence to really grow up and be independent? I'm too tied to you, so this way I can fake it." Does that sound about right, is that what he says?

Mother: Absolutely not. He doesn't talk like that—he's disrespectful. And he's not tied to me.

Interviewer: Oh, OK, I see. Disrespectful, I see. How about this. "Dammit, Mom, you never even let me wash behind my ears myself. If it wasn't for Pop getting mad and forcing me to be responsible sometimes, I'd never grow up!" Does that sound more like it?

The first statement was made to Mom, primarily for the benefit of Johnny, who had chosen not to participate. He might hear in this context what I'd otherwise never be able to say to him. The second statement was made to Mom, primarily for Pop's benefit, since he's rarely exerted himself to discipline Johnny in the face of Mom's protectiveness. I would never try to make such points directly, so playing the role gives me the chance. Also, since I'm doing such a lousy job and saying such foolish things, Johnny might change his mind and take over the role.

Some of these last ideas show how difficult I find it to refrain from throwing in a few therapy shots in a session. But a planted seed may grow someday, and the moves help to facilitate the role playing, to build rapport and alter perceptions, and to derive more data for assessing.

In this example of role playing, the family had refused to focus and Pop and Johnny were relatively uncommunicative. Role playing will frequently open up an uncommunicative family—it is an action-oriented technique. It makes a vague family become specific. It also usually works well with a family that is just too emotional, screaming at each other throughout a session. There I introduce the technique "because I want to get *exactly* clear what happens." Then, the role playing serves to distance the family from what they were discussing; they can act through the same thing less emotionally, especially with the assistance of my frequent interruptions and directions. In these cases, making the interruption while monitoring and directing the role playing is easier than doing so during the heated discussion. On occasion, the role playing itself escalates emotion; then I just stop it and try something else.

Role playing can thus be used to get a withdrawn family usefully involved or to help an overly emotional family gain some distance and calm down. It can also be used to get more specific information. The other benefit of the role-playing technique is that, when it works, it's a lot of fun.

Chapter Six

Planning, Designing Tasks, and Helping Clients Take Action

Ideally, Step 3 merges into Step 4 as a plan evolves rather naturally from the definition of the problem and the assessment of Aquilera and Messick's lists. The worker develops a tentative long-range plan aimed at correcting some of the inadequacies of perception, supportive network, and coping mechanisms, which thus leads to resolution of the problem.

The worker also makes short-range plans, which include the short-range goals for the clients to accomplish both in the particular session and afterwards. These plans include the worker's goals for the session and his intended plan of man-

125

agement of the session. The general goals of the first session usually include the first five steps of crisis intervention—establishing communication and rapport, assessing the problem, assessing resources and strengths, planning, and mobilizing. Within that framework, more specific goals must be established—for example, to establish rapport with Father, to get Mother and Grandpa speaking to each other again, or to get Joe to agree to participate in whatever task is chosen for the family. The plans must specify then how the worker intends to accomplish these goals. The various goals are an integral part of the overall plan and should ultimately be formulated in terms that are specific, measurable, and behavioral in nature.

Goals can be thought of in general terms and then broken down into specific measurable components. If the overall long-range goal is improved communication in the marriage, the first short-range goal might be for the wife to tell the husband what she learns when she calls the school tomorrow, and the specific long-range goal might be that she keep him informed on a weekly basis of their son's accomplishments and problems in school, "since we all know that fathers are interested in keeping tabs on their son's progress in school even though in most families, especially ones where the father works as hard as this one, the mothers usually handle anything that comes up."

To a large extent, most of these plans and goals will be the worker's and not be discussed. This is especially true of the long-range goals and plans. Also, I very rarely use the terms *goal* and *plan* with a family during crisis intervention; instead, especially at first, I tend to talk more about what might be tried tomorrow and, depending on how that goes, what might be considered for next week. Thus, I might suggest that someone call an agency to see if they offer certain services without ever directly suggesting that they use those services. I will occasionally mention "after this works out" or "a few years from now" to help instill hope and shift perspective, but that has nothing to do with the planning.

Plans might be cautiously shared with the family to the degree that they can tolerate them, and the best plans are those that unfold naturally and collaboratively as we discuss the trouble and the chain of events that led to it. In general, I will try to incorporate any ideas or suggestions the family can come up with, unless they seem definitely untherapeutic, such as seeming doomed to failure or aimed at gaining vengeance or victory over another family member.

Interviewer: Well, Mr. Jones, you were pretty upset about your mother, and then when you learned your wife had a tumor you thought she'd die right away, like the worst thing that could happen, and then you didn't know of anywhere you could get help with the kids. That's when it just seemed too much, and you left for a while. Then, of course your wife was furious when you got back and things really fell apart between you and got even worse after you hit her.

Mr. Jones: Yeah. I knew I couldn't help her and work and take care of the kids, too, and then when I got back we couldn't even talk anymore. And I don't really even know what's really wrong with her.

Interviewer: Yeah. Mrs. Jones, when the doctor talked to you, you got so scared, and you weren't sure what he was saying after you heard "tumor"?

Mrs. Jones: Uh huh. He was talking so fast. If only he could explain it to my husband. Jim always understands things quicker than I do anyway.

Mr. Jones: Well, he explained pretty good when she had that hyster-thing operation. Maybe I could call him.

Interviewer: That sounds like an idea. Do you think he'd really sit down and talk to both of you together like that? [Implying that going to see the doctor together was Jim's idea]

Here The Problem is that the family has not yet adjusted to the wife having a tumor. Their perceptions of the situation are based on unverified assumptions and are interfering with their functioning. The husband's inadequate perception is that his wife is going to die almost immediately and that there is no way he can cope without her. Her inadequate perception is that he left because he doesn't care about her and didn't want to be bothered. I tried to correct this by merely outlining the chain of events, without even saying anything about it directly. I could have used plussing, but it wasn't necessary. The network is inadequate because his mother died recently, they've no close family, they don't know about services offered by agencies or the cancer society, they live somewhat seclusively and haven't yet thought about turning to friends and neighbors, and they haven't been supporting each other. Their coping mechanisms are inadequate because neither has had to face anything like the threat of her dying, because the idea came as a total surprise, because he's still at a low ebb from losing his mother, and because the option of relying on his mother's concrete help and emotional support is no longer available.

If they go see her doctor together, they will be supporting each other. The doctor may perceive the upset and become more supportive. Perceptions will be clarified and become more factual—the tumor may not be serious, and if it is, they can find out more definitely what to expect. If they leave this first session intending to call the doctor, then they have a plan and a task and are mobilized in a problem-solving effort. I also hope in this first session to find a way that they might get a short, immediate break from the kids. One possibility is the kids spending the next two afternoons with a woman from church. The long-range plan is, if necessary, to begin to hook the couple up with the cancer society and social services, as well as exploring further supportive resources, such as church and neighbors.

These clients will leave the session with at least one *task*, that is, to call about an appointment with the doctor. The use of tasks is an important technique in crisis intervention and serves many functions. The task is like homework, something the clients will do before the next session. It focuses their attention and efforts, and it helps to organize a chaotic situation. The client's have a specific, concrete action they can do, actively working toward solving their own problem. They no longer feel helpless and are no longer immobile. The task is a major tool in Step 5, in *mobilizing* the clients in a specific direction and in a purposeful way. This changes the clients' self-image and their perception of the whole situation. The focus is shifted from tension reduction to problem solving. Accomplishing the task is as important as what is accomplished. That is, ideally the task will be a step in the process of resolving The Problem, but even if the task does not bear directly upon it, having a task and accomplishing it constitute an important early step in the intervention.

In selecting a task, it is nice when an idea evolves naturally from discussing the situation, especially if the idea comes from the clients themselves, and it is nice when the task bears a clear relationship to resolving The Problem. All of this occurred when Mr. and Mrs. Jones somewhat mutually suggested calling the doctor. That was an ideal and unusual occurrence, however. Frequently, unless he has been able to guide or modify the clients' ideas, the worker must choose the task himself. This still is best done by leading the clients into the task rather than imposing it on them.

It is most important that the task selected be one that the clients will *do*. This requires that the worker utilize both imaginative thinking and careful reading of the clients. It is also extremely important that the task selected, especially the first task, be one in which the client will succeed. Careful attention to wording can be a critical factor. For example, the Joneses' task would be to call the doctor to ask if he will see them. They would probably do this; thus, success is built in. They might even go further and actually see the doctor. If the task had been to call the doctor and make an appointment, they might fail—he might be booked up or even refuse to see them. If the task had been to see the doctor, there is an even greater chance of failure. In order to turn the crisis process around, it is essential that the client have an initial success.

The task should make some sense to the clients; they should feel that it relates directly to whatever is troubling them, even though the worker need not necessarily share that feeling. The task should be a large enough feat to seem significant but small enough that it doesn't seem too difficult. It should be both specific and measurable—"Call and answer two help-wanted ads from the Sunday *Sun* this week" rather than "check the classified ads"; "Call social services and see if they'll give you an appointment to discuss this foster care problem" rather than "Make an appointment with social services"; or perhaps "Let's see, then, by Thursday you're going to ask your wife if she's willing to make a budget with you this weekend" rather than "Make a budget with your wife."

To further ensure that the client will actually do the task, I try to convey, without saying "I'll check up on you," that I will follow up ("OK, then, I'll call you Thursday night and see how it went."). It can be useful to have the task agreed to in front of others or even to involve others in the task ("OK, if Jim's going to call the doctor, then Mary, would you call me Thursday morning about nine to let me know where things stand?" It can help to let the clients see me write the task down, showing that I take it seriously and intend to follow up on it. Similarly, I may write something about it—a phone number to call, someone's name, or part of the task itself—on a card and give it to the clients.

Another aid in ensuring that the task is performed is *anticipatory planning*—a technique useful in several aspects of crisis intervention. Simply put, anticipatory planning means anticipating with the client things that might go wrong and tentatively planning how they might be dealt with. This has two benefits: First, the client will not leave feeling that all his problems are solved and expecting smooth sailing, ready to be thrown for a loop when the first obstacle arises. If we have anticipated an obstacle that he encounters, he will already have a plan for dealing with it that will make things much easier; if not, at least we will have rehearsed a problem-solving approach to obstacles and he will be expecting a problem instead of being caught by surprise. Second, anticipatory planning functions as something of a paradoxical maneuver that can leave the client arguing with me that he *can* do something rather than arguing that he can't; this markedly increases the chances that he will do it. This happens because rather than having the client voice his objections and fears regarding the task as I offer encouragement, solutions, and reassurance, I reverse the process. I try to anticipate and raise his objections and fears before he can, and then I set up a problem-solving approach to deal with the problems.

Interviewer:	So, what will you do if the doctor won't give you an appointment?
Mr. Jones:	Gee, I don't know. Why would he do that?
Interviewer:	I don't know, but if he does, what'll you do then?
Mr. Jones:	I don't know. Maybe I could call another doctor?
Interviewer:	Do you mean like to ask for a consultation?
Mr. Jones:	Yeah, that's it.
Interviewer:	That might work. What if you call the doctor and he's on vacation for a week, what'll you do then?
Interviewer:	So you can call social services, and ask what their rules are for getting homemaker services. Now, of course you know you'll probably get put on hold, or transferred to three different people, or the right person will be on vacation.
Interviewer:	Now you know you're likely to get very embarrassed asking the doctor for another appointment when you've just seen him for this. If you're embarrassed, how will you handle that?
Mrs. Jones:	Yeah, that's right, I hadn't really thought about that. Oh. [Pause.] Well, I guess I *am* paying him, though.
Mr. Jones:	Look, don't worry about it. You want me to call him?

I have learned the hard way never to tell anyone what someone else *is* going to do, even if I have a promise in writing and signed. Instead, I apply the principle of anticipatory planning:

Interviewer: Dr. Murphy *says* if you call on Tuesday, he'll see you.

Anticipatory planning is useful at various points of the work, particularly with Step 5, mobilizing, and Step 6, closing. During the middle phase of the work, it can be used to shift focus and put the problem in perspective. For example, if the parents have complaints about the behavior of fifteen-year-old Buddy, I might ask how they plan to handle his twelve-year-old sister, Bunny, when she begins to get rebellious, or what they think they'll do if Buddy wants to marry a girl they don't approve of. Near closing, with the crisis resolved or nearly so, I will begin anticipating with the family difficulties that will soon be arising as they work on their problems after the termination ("Now, you know sometimes these workers in juvenile services get switched to different assignments. What'll you do if all of a sudden James gets assigned a new worker?"). I will also anticipate with them future problems that might arise after the current batch is resolved ("Now after Johnny gets back on the track, I guess that'll be about time Dad'll be worrying about retirement?"). Finally, at the followup phone call, I'll frequently mention a future problem. This anticipatory planning helps prepare the family so they can see that life naturally consists of a never ending series of problems, and it reduces the tendency for the family to react to each problem as a crisis which should not have occurred, which implies that they are failures, and which must be someone's fault.

If the initial work with the clients has gone well, then rapport has been established, they feel some hope, and they have shifted to a problem-solving focus. If the problem and chain of events have unfolded well, then a well-chosen task will appeal to them. It should be carefully presented. I frequently present it as an experiment ("Let's try this and see what happens"), which helps structure the situation so there can be no failure—the goal is to see what happens. The task is then reinforced by the various methods described. With a favorable combination of all of these factors, it is most likely that the task will be done, and done successfully. I emphasize that one major reason it will be done successfully is that it was specifically chosen and defined with that aim in mind.

I do not try to get people to do something they don't want to do. If they show hesitation, I back off. In such a situation, I use paradox:

Interviewer: Now, Mr. Jones, I don't want you to get involved in talking to the social worker. If you can manage to keep handling that job of yours, I think that's plenty load enough for one man.

If Mr. Jones agrees with me, then nothing is lost, and maybe I will think of something else he can do. If he disagrees with me, I may let him argue me into agreeing that he might be able to call the social worker after all. The odds are then much higher that he will do it than if I try to argue him into it, getting his resentful and ambivalent agreement. By approaching the idea this way, I protect my power, which would be lost if I pushed him into agreeing and then he didn't do it.

If I learn on my checkup phone call or on their return visit that the clients haven't done the task, something is badly awry. I have no highly effective way to deal with this. It is difficult to recoup the resultant loss of power, rapport, and movement. First, I will inquire what happened. Infrequently I learn there was some simple problem—a misunderstanding or a coincidence—which presented an obstacle; such a situation can usually be resolved easily.

Usually, though, I get a rather feeble excuse or a complaint ("I decided it wouldn't help."). I always accept the excuse. I usually try more paradox then ("Yeah, I can see we picked something too hard—I probably should have realized how upset you were. Maybe you'll prefer a smaller step to start with."). Sometimes I commiserate about the lost opportunity

("Gee, that's too bad. We've missed a chance to see how that would turn out.").

Of course, I do not chastise, plead, or reason with the clients, and I rarely confront them. The simplest approach is to avoid making a big deal of the failure and to proceed with the session while internally trying to figure out the reason the task wasn't done. Hopefully, a better task can be chosen for this session. I occasionally try to figure out a paradoxical task—I ask them to do more of what they're already doing or do something that I'm sure they will not do (hoping that their counter-reactions will mobilize them and increase my power again):

"Look, I'm sorry, I was trying to get you to move too fast. Maybe what you need is some rest. For the next three days don't think about this problem at all. Don't try to think of anything you might do—anyone you might call or talk to, or anywhere you might go to improve things. It may be better to just not try to think about it, and above all, don't try to *do* anything. Don't discuss any of this with each other, just rest. Then I'll call you Friday afternoon and see how you're doing."

The beauty of such a paradoxical task is that the clients may "obey" me by doing nothing, which increases my power. Or, they may push against me and do something—which is what I want. Unfortunately, these paradoxical moves don't actually work very well for me, but I occasionally try them if stumped and if dealing with a family which seems resistive, especially passive-resistive, and which seems to be highly motivated to thwart me.

Sometimes the clients fail due to my misjudgment or some coincidence rather than their passive resistance. This creates a setback in the clients' self-image, hope, and movement, as well as weakening my power. While this is troublesome and undesirable, it is less disruptive to the intervention process and less ominous in terms of the clients' workability than the situation in which they just don't attempt the task. When their genuine attempts are unsuccessful, the reasons must be understood in a manner similar to establishing the chain of events, and the clients need empathic support. This failure basically represents and is dealt with as a minicrisis occurring within the larger crisis intervention process.

The very best way to deal with uncompleted tasks is to avoid their occurrence entirely—carefully choose the original task so that the clients will try it and succeed. Then mobilization will occur.

In summary, the mobilizing step begins with the first contact, and many of the procedures and processes of the intervention stimulate and maintain the clients' motivation and movement. Merely having a session assists in this, as does the use of the relationship, support, enhancing the self-image, the shift to thinking and problem solving, and the action-oriented focus. The primary factor in enhancing mobilization is the skillful use of tasks. Assessing, planning, and mobilizing are not separate processes. In the course of evaluating the problem and unfolding the chain of events, a plan of action naturally evolves; with a plan, the clients begin to be mobilized. The problem and the plan suggest a task, which is then used to further the mobilization and to ensure that it is carried on beyond the session.

Bargaining is a technique generally more suited to therapy than to crisis intervention, but it's very useful when it's needed for the latter. This occurs most often during developmental crises. Developmental crises, such as those evolving from a youngster's adolescence, usually result in personal and family strains that often lead to an escalating process of power moves and countermoves and they sometimes lead to nearly insurmountable obstacles to reconciliation. The family can appear for crisis intervention apparently deadlocked in a struggle over various concrete issues, which in fact reflect the underlying, more basic issues of separation, autonomy, rivalry, and power. In such situations, bargaining is most often needed. Father will not let Diane date Bart; she dates him anyway; she can't live at home if she won't follow rules; that's all right, she and Bart (age seventeen) are planning to get an apartment anyway; and besides, she thinks she might be pregnant.

Bargaining may break the deadlock when nothing else

will. It may also cool off the crisis or at least buy some time, although in itself it is unlikely to resolve the underlying developmental problem.

Interviewer: Diane, you said you wanted Dad to just meet Bart.

Diane: Right, he says he's a hippy punk, but . . . .

Interviewer: OK. Dad, you've never met him?

Dad: I don't need to meet any hippy to know . . . .

Interviewer: OK, you've never met him. You want Diane to stop dating him.

Diane: He's got no reason, he's just stubborn, and . . . .

Interviewer: Well, he's got *his* reasons, whatever, he can't sleep when you're out, and long hair upsets him, right? So, how long could you go without dating Bart?

Diane: Why should I? There's nothing wrong with him!

Interviewer: OK, Bart's fine with you. Right. But how long *could* you go without a date with him? I mean, without dying, you know, how long could you exist?

Diane: I don't know, a week, I don't know.

Interviewer: OK, a week you could exist without a date with Bart. How about two weeks?

Diane: No!

Dad: That's ridiculous, can't exist without . . . .

Interviewer: OK, but Diane says she can't exist two weeks without a date with Bart. Not two weeks, how about ten days?

Diane: I don't know, maybe, but why should I give up . . . .

Interviewer: OK, OK, ten days maybe. Dad, you said Diane's out every night. If she'd go ten days without dating him, would you be willing to meet him?

Dad: I don't *need* to meet him, I *know* what kind of . . . .

Interviewer: OK, yeah, you don't *need* to meet him, OK, but would you be *willing* to meet him if Diane didn't date him for ten days?

Dad: Yeah, OK, I could, but I still wouldn't let her date him.

Interviewer: OK, but she's dating him every night now, you said, so you'll meet him if she'll stop dating him for ten days. How about that, Diane?

Diane: Ten days is a long time; that's too long. No.

Interviewer: Ten days is too long. How about nine days if Dad will meet him?

Diane: No.

Interviewer: No. OK, how about eight, eight days?

Diane: Maybe.

Interviewer: OK, Dad, how about that? Will you meet him if she doesn't date him for eight days?

Dad: No. Ten days.

Interviewer: Diane, Dad says no, ten days.

Diane: No.

Interviewer: Ten days is too long. What if you see him but not date him?

Diane: What do you mean?

Interviewer: Like see him, like at home?

Dad: No, I won't have that hippy punk over at my house all hours of the day and night when I'm not there, and they . . . .

Interviewer: OK, Dad, OK, what about while you are there?

Dad: No, I don't want him around.

Interviewer: Well, could you stand it at all? How about an hour?

Dad: Why should I have to put up with some . . . .

Interviewer: Sure, OK, but if Diane wasn't going out with him, could you stand him at the house an hour?

Dad: They couldn't sneak around in the bedroom or something; he'd probably head right for the bedroom.

Interviewer: Well, what? The living room?

Dad: Family room.

Interviewer: OK, family room. Diane, could you stand not dating Bart for two weeks if your Dad would meet him *and* you could see him an hour once a week?

Diane: No, that's not enough.

Interviewer: Not enough. What about twice a week?

Diane: Two weeks is too long.

Interviewer: What about ten days, if you saw him twice and Dad met him?

Diane: OK.

Interviewer: Dad, how about that?

Dad: How do I know if I'd let him visit, I haven't met him?

The bargain finally reached was this:

Agreement between Diane Burns and
Mr. and Mrs. A. J. Burns 9/13/77

1. It is hereby agreed that Diane will remain home to live under the following conditions:
   a. She agrees she will not date Bart for four days. *Date* means to be in the presence of, outside the home. Phone calls are not restricted.
   b. During that time, Dad will meet Bart. Diane will arrange this. Dad will be available either Tuesday or Thursday night between 7 and 9 P.M.
   c. If Dad *then* agrees, Diane will not date Bart for six more days, and Diane and Bart may visit in the family

room, with the door open, for not more than one hour, two evenings when Dad is home. Diane may choose any two evenings, except Friday night. Dad agrees to be home every other evening except Friday.

2. On the ninth day of this contract, Dad, Mom, and Diane will meet with Dr. Puryear to discuss further plans.
3. Mom agrees to notify Dad within one hour or as soon as possible if she becomes aware of Diane violating this contract in any way.
4. This contract may be freely canceled by any of the three parties by merely notifying the other two at any time. Diane agrees to call Dr. Puryear within three hours if this occurs.
5. This contract goes into effect as of now, 11 A.M., 9/13/77. It is automatically void at 8 A.M., 9/23/77.

After arriving at this agreement, I read the terms to the three parties and asked if each believed that this was what they had agreed to and if each was willing to follow it or required any changes. I first used the word *contract* during this reading; the family then realized what was going on—that there was really more to this than just talk—but by then they were somewhat committed. They agreed that this was what they had agreed to, and I then took my notes to my secretary. She quickly typed the contract on the official stationery of the Office of the Court Psychiatrist, Circuit Court of Baltimore County; we all signed it; and each of us got a copy of our own. The session was wrapped up quickly thereafter, and Diane and her parents went home.

They did not follow the contract in various ways, there was a minor blowup, and Diane eventually left home. However, she left some days *after* the blowup, in a rather calm fashion, and with the reluctant agreement and assistance of her parents. We could say this leaving represented a partial resolution of the crisis. It was certainly healthier than the damaging, tension-discharging, kicked-out/stormed-out process that was evolving before the bargaining.

The bargaining bought some time. It gave the family an opportunity to relate to each other in a different way—with guarded cooperativeness rather than total authoritarianism or total defiance. This gave them a chance to talk and work together to minimize the losses that were going to occur. And it helped resolve the crisis (or at least the impending crisis) situation.

I follow a number of principles in the bargaining technique that seem to make it work best for me:

1. I ease into *doing* bargaining without talking about it. I use the clients' complaints and wishes, act as a go-between, and just ask if they'll agree. I do not take it upon myself to bring them to agreement or to push anyone to agree to anything or to change their position. Rather, I function as the mediator and keep offering alternatives. If we reach an impasse or stalemate, I just say so and leave it in their laps ("OK, we've got those positions clear. What do you want to do now?").

2. As much as possible, I seek agreements that *minimize* the compromise aspect, that is, minimize the amount of ground anyone gives up. In the example above, Diane is giving up the dating but only temporarily, but Dad is giving up *nothing* that he actually *has*—though he relaxes somewhat his ineffective determination to prevent Diane's involvement with Bart. Again, I do not try to persuade but just state the option ("She says she'll do this if you'll do that."). At most, I sometimes point out reluctantly that this is not a compromise, that no one is giving up anything they really have—but I do this only as a last resort ("Well, Mr. Burns, this certainly isn't what you want, but how does it stack up with what you have? With how things are going now?" or "This *isn't* what you want. Could you live with this?").

3. I totally accept everyone's viewpoint, without judgment. If Johnny is determined to shave his head and paint it with fluorescent green paint, I may not understand it, but I accept that as his wish, for his reasons, whatever they may be—and I don't even inquire what they are. We may then be able to bargain, and he'll settle for just painting his ears if his mother will change her demand that he be in the house by 7 P.M. every night—which I also don't question ("Sure,

Johnny, I understand. From your viewpoint, you're perfectly able to take care of yourself even if you stay out all night, but here it is, somehow your mother can't sleep while you're out.").

4. These comments don't apply if someone is not bargaining in good faith. He may do this in several ways: by not budging on any point, by agreeing to anything at all with no intention of following through, or by initially pushing unreasonable demands merely for the purpose of having more bargaining power. It usually quickly becomes clear when someone is doing this. Now, they are under no obligation to bargain in good faith—I never asked them to and they never agreed to. I usually point out what is happening, and if they won't shift, I let it go. It merely means the bargaining technique won't work, and something else must be tried.

A variant of not bargaining in good faith arises when someone continues to bargain while steadfastly maintaining—and sometimes with good reason—that the *other* person is not bargaining in good faith.

Mother: OK, that's all right with me, nine o'clock. What difference does it make, she agrees now but she won't do any of this. She's always making promises.

I have three options at that point. First, I may try putting in the escape clause (which I was going to put in anyway):

Interviewer: Look, Mom, you're getting yourself in a corner, agreeing to these things when you don't trust her. Look, would it be better for you if we said you can agree, but you can call all the agreements off anytime you want? How would that be?

Or I may try paradox:

Interviewer: Look, Mom, this really isn't a good idea. I mean, here you are agreeing, but you're sure she won't

> follow through. It must seem hopeless to you.
> You just can't trust her at all. Wouldn't it be
> better if you just didn't agree to these things?

Or I may just drop bargaining and try something else, as I would if the first two options didn't work out.

Any of these ways of not bargaining in good faith suggest a poor prognosis and a difficult situation, indicating that the nonamenable person will likely not be an asset, although he might respond to some other approach.

5. When people are bargaining in good faith, I try to protect them from bad agreements. This gives them more confidence in the process and enhances their cooperativeness, since they don't feel so pushed into things. It certainly increases the chances that they will follow the agreement. And, it is a nice paradoxical move—it makes me even less responsible for obtaining an agreement ("Hold on, John, you just agreed you'd mow the yard every weekend for a dollar. But you said it's a big yard; are you going to be satisfied with that? I mean, there you are, Saturday afternoon, all sweating and hot, and you're thinking, 'One dollar?' Are you sure about that?" Or "Dad, wait, look, you said you'd take him to the ball games if he'd wax the car. But you didn't say *when* he'd wax the car or how often. What if he decides he'll do it either next Christmas or the one after that? If you were a union negotiator, would you agree to a vague provision like that?").

6. Once the bargaining starts, I try to get people to stick with it. As in role playing, they will frequently try to revert to "Let me tell you what she did last year," and I must say "OK, but right now I was trying to find out if you could live with a ten o'clock curfew now?"

7. The provisions of the agreement must be as specific as possible. For example, if "John agrees to help clean up the house," we need to specify what, when, and how much. Better, then, is "John agrees to wash the dishes Tuesday and Thursday night before 9 P.M. and to vacuum the entire first floor on Saturday by 5 P.M., except when he has a baseball game, when he'll do it by Sunday at 1 P.M." I try to be very active and

imaginative in figuring out all possible loopholes ("How will you know if he really has a baseball game? You'll believe him if he says so?" Or "John, what if they leave the dishes all weekend and Monday for you to do Tuesday? Should we say 'do the day's dishes'?"). Now, I can't possibly think of all the loopholes, but I hope to catch most of the major and most tempting ones. I then use this process to point out to the clients that anyone can sabotage the contract very easily if they want to. For example, John can wash the dishes in a style that breaks half of them and leaves egg on the other half. Or Mom can say the dishes aren't clean enough, no matter how he does them. It is impossible to anticipate every possibility.

8. This leads to the next point: These contracts *never* work. That is, in my experience, I have never worked out a contract and had everyone return happy, with everyone having done what they agreed to. Usually someone has sabotaged it somewhere, gotten mad about something else and either retaliated by rejecting the contract or begun to brood about "having to make agreements with some punk kid." Or, at the very least, someone just found that he had agreed to something that he really wasn't willing to do. Therefore I build into each contract provisions for termination and renegotiation. This means that once the contract is violated or junked, the whole concept is not necessarily rejected in angry frustration as it otherwise would be. Sometimes part of the next session can be used for renegotiating if it seems desirable. Sometimes, as in the Diane Burns example, the contract doesn't work, but it helps get the crisis resolved.

It might be tempting to think of bargaining as a vehicle for therapy, wherein people deal with each other rationally and the real issues and problems are worked out through negotiation. I have not found that to occur. I do find bargaining useful in crisis intervention to break up a deadlock in a session where I can see no other alternative, and it is also useful for calming things down and buying some time. Bargaining enables people to talk with each other, provides some structure, and may be a vehicle where people can experience their relationship in a different way and with a different viewpoint. It would be nice to think that these things might be beneficial in themselves and that someone might use the bargaining process as a model for resolving future conflicts.

Bargaining might seem useful in a variety of situations, for example, marital conflict. I personally find, however, that it is usually only of value to me in the parent-adolescent situations I have described. Some people claim that bargaining undermines parental authority. I see bargaining as a way of exercising parental authority; the parents do not have to agree to anything they don't want to. Furthermore, I use bargaining primarily in situations where parental authority seems lost anyway—frequently the parents either were never firm enough to establish any authority or were rigidly authoritarian and unable to become more flexible as the child grew older, resulting in the adolescent's rejection of their authority after an escalating series of power struggles. Authority cannot be undermined where it doesn't exist.

Chapter Seven

Closing the Intervention and Following Up

After the first session or two, when the important early work has been done and the task assigned, there is sometimes little left to do. If all goes well, the clients will do the task and go on from there. They may even do more than the task assigned. They sometimes call to say they don't really need the next session, thank you. This outcome stems from the worker's skill and creativity in establishing rapport, assessing and evaluating, defining The Problem, formulating a plan, choosing a task, and mobilizing. Of course, it also depends on such factors as the nature of the situation, the family's assets, and luck.

Often the crisis situation doesn't resolve so quickly, and more work must be done. This begins the "midgame" phase of the intervention. There must be a continuation of maintenance work and the steps of planning and mobilizing as the clients reach one goal and move on to the next. At each step obstacles may arise; these must be recognized, evaluated, and overcome. Plans and goals may have to be reassessed and changed. However, crises don't last over six weeks, and the goal of resolution will be reached, although all of the specific component subgoals may not be accomplished within that time.

The midgame is similar to and employs the same principles as the first part of the work. In midgame sessions the worker should focus largely on the here-and-now. Questions of history, feelings, and direction dealt with in the earlier work should not be reopened. The worker needs to keep firmly in mind the definition of The Problem and his basic plan, including the series of desired goals. Although the short-range plans and goals may be altered, changes in the basic plan and in the definition of The Problem should be avoided; if changes are necessary, they should be made smoothly, subtly, and gradually rather than abruptly or radically. The primary format of the session should be reviewing the results of the task and determining the next task. The next task should be assigned, mobilizing work should be done as necessary, the next session or followup arranged, and the session ended. If the work is proceeding reasonably well, further sessions, if needed, are spaced increasingly further apart and are briefer. Often phone calls can be used instead of sessions. This tapering off process gradually reduces support while increasing the clients' self-reliance; it gradually merges into and facilitates the closing process, and it conserves the worker's time. The format of crisis intervention calls for a *maximum* of six sessions plus a few phone calls, requiring a maximum of eight hours of the worker's time. Most cases will be resolved in much less time. Step 6, closing, should begin early and should hinge on crisis resolution, not on the absence of problems or turmoil. At closure, the clients will hopefully be engaged in some constructive work on their problems that they were *not* doing when they were in crisis.

When things go well, the midgame almost takes care of

itself. When they don't go so well, the midgame requires more effort and can be difficult. Within the task-focused session, the worker will have to deal with various obstacles. The possible difficulties are varied and legion. They range from the severe—the clients didn't attempt the task, the husband refuses to come to the next session as agreed, Johnny ran away again—to the mild—the clients introduce arguments and concerns that hinder the crisis intervention process, the clients attempted the task and didn't succeed, or they succeeded but did not pick up enough momentum to continue on their own. These various difficulties should be handled with the methods previously described—active listening, paradox, support, and so on—and attention should return to the basic plan and to the next task as soon as possible.

Crisis intervention is action oriented, suited to dealing with circumscribed and rather acute problems. It is not particularly suited for exploring and resolving deep, chronic, complex issues, such as a chronic power struggle between husband and wife, a weakness or lack of authority or structure within a family, or a mother's chronic rejection of a child resulting from her transference-based misperceptions. The exploring and working out of such issues are in the province of therapy, and usually rather lengthy therapy. When such issues *must* be dealt with in crisis intervention, they are generally not explored or even discussed, but addressed through a task that is designed to change the manner in which the issue is expressed in the family. If therapy is indicated and desired, referring the family for therapy or negotiating a new contract for obtaining it from the crisis worker can be done as part of the crisis work. Such movement from crisis intervention to therapy is rare—as it should be. It will not work out for most crisis cases. Careful evaluation and preparation should be used before such an action is made.

At midgame, there can be a particularly strong pull to do therapy—to solve the family's problems, to deal with the basic issues—and it can be difficult to stick to the original goal of crisis resolution with (hopefully) some growth. The task-focused format helps the worker avoid getting involved in the interesting and tempting but extraneous pursuit of therapy, which can lead to a confused, unstructured, time-consuming morass. Such an erroneous course usually ends with the crisis being resolved within a context of frustration, loose ends, and unresolved issues. At that point the worker may have the family unwillingly involved in an unplanned and unfocused therapy, or perhaps the intervention may terminate with the process having stirred up trouble and planted seeds for the next crisis. Or the crisis may be resolved at a less healthy level of functioning than might have otherwise been accomplished.

Following is an excerpt from a midgame session:

Interviewer:	So, Mr. Jones, when the doctor told you your wife not only has cancer but has a particularly bad kind, that really hit you hard.
Mr. Jones:	Yeah.
Interviewer:	Even though that's what you thought, or feared, hearing it for real was still a shock.
Mr. Jones:	Yeah.
Interviewer:	So you really haven't been in a condition to do a lot of thinking or planning since our last meeting—you got this meeting with the doctor, and it takes a while to digest something like that.
Mr. Jones:	Yeah. Well, I did talk to the neighbor.
Interviewer:	To the neighbor?
Mr. Jones:	Yeah. She said her sister had something like this and needed a special bed, or something. And she said she could watch the kids while I work.
Interviewer:	She'll watch the kids?
Mr. Jones:	Yeah, but she wants $5 a day, she said.
Mrs. Jones:	Oh, we can't afford that!
Interviewer:	That really would add up.

Mr. Jones:	Yeah. I don't know, she might do it for nothing for a little while, maybe. Or maybe I could do something to trade off, like.
Interviewer:	You said you do mechanic work on the side sometimes?
Mr. Jones:	Yeah, they've got two cars over there, I don't know how they're running—but I think one of her boys works on them sometimes. Maybe he could use some help though; he's just a young kid.
Interviewer:	So you've got some ideas there to check into.
Mr. Jones:	Yeah.
Interviewer:	Did the doctor say anything about a special bed, or equipment or anything?
Mr. Jones:	No, I don't think so. He talked so fast, you know. But he said she'd be down at home for a while after surgery.
Interviewer:	So you're wondering how that'll be.
Mr. Jones:	Yeah, the neighbor said it was pretty rough for a while with her sister.
Interviewer:	So you're kinda worried, wonder how that'll be.
Mr. Jones:	Yeah. Her sister died.
Interviewer:	That's pretty scary. That's a scary part, for both of you.
Mr. and Mrs. Jones:	Yeah.
Interviewer:	Have you two talked much about these things yet?
Mr. Jones:	[in obvious distress] Well, you know, I don't want to upset her and all.
Interviewer:	[still pushing the idea of talking] Yeah. Sometimes the talking goes better a little bit at a time. [Now shifting away before

more resistance builds up] So, the immediate things, what's on your mind is the kids and maybe some equipment.

Mr. Jones: Yeah.

Interviewer: Did your doctor mention anything about the cancer society?

Mr. Jones: No. What're they, research and stuff?

Interviewer: Well, you know, you've probably donated to them before sometime — I think they have different programs — like maybe they loan equipment, stuff like that. [I *know* they loan equipment, but I don't know for sure that they'll loan it to the Joneses, and I want the idea of using the cancer society to come from the Joneses as much as possible.]

Mr. Jones: Well, maybe I should call them.

Interviewer: Well, OK. Here's one of my cards; you've got a pen there? Let's see if the number is in the phone book here. [(1) If he already has the number, he's more likely to call; (2) I certainly don't want him to get frustrated later on trying to find the number — he's a good mechanic but not a strong reader — and I'm not sure what it's listed under; (3) he's doing part of the work here and yet I am giving him something — the number and the card; (4) so far, *calling* is *his* idea and his business — it's no skin off my nose if he doesn't.]

Interviewer: So, let's see, Mr. Jones, you're going to see about this neighbor and the kids, some kind of trade-off maybe, and you're calling the cancer society Monday or Tuesday to see what kind of programs they have and if they lend equipment. And they'll call me if they aren't clear about the situation or if you run into problems. [A bad move, undermining his competence and independence, but maybe necessary to avoid his getting too frustrated with bureaucratic hassles that I don't think he's ready for and to short-circuit the agency asking them to come for interviews like we've just had. This is anticipatory planning.] And Mrs. Jones, you're going to ask two neighbors about anyone else in the neighborhood that keeps kids. So, I'll call you Tuesday night—OK?—to see what you've got. And why don't we plan to meet in about ten days from now to go over where things stand. Maybe take half an hour. Mr. Jones, you said you can get off work a little early on Wednesdays or Fridays?

So this is midgame, the second session with Mr. and Mrs. Jones. It lasted forty minutes (I had fifty scheduled) and took place five days after the first session, which lasted one hour and ten minutes (I had one and a half hours scheduled). The crisis intervention was arranged after Mr. Jones had walked out on his family and then hit his wife during the row following his return. They did the task of calling the doctor to see about an appointment and went further—they actually had it. They got the bad news—Mr. Jones' perception of his wife's condition turned out to be pretty accurate, though it still was inadequate because it was based on overreactive fears rather than on factual data. Now he had factual data and a better understanding of the situation—but it was too much and he was rather overwhelmed. He didn't do much, and Mrs. Jones gave him some comfort, but then he *did* talk to the neighbor—thus expanding the network and beginning more problem solving. If I can shift the Joneses to a worker at the cancer society for the long haul ahead, I will. This crisis is now almost resolved. I will stay in touch with them and be available for the next crisis, which seems to have a fair chance of occurring. My short-range goal of getting them to start dealing with the practical problems has been just about achieved. My long-range goal of helping them face the hard facts and support each other through improved communication has a way to go and may never be accomplished. The short- and long-range goals of increasing the supportive network seems to be developing satisfactorily.

Closing, although the sixth step, actually begins with opening. I usually say in the first session or at its end that we'll meet a "few times" to see what can be worked out. Closing begins in earnest as I begin decreasing the frequency and length of the sessions. If we have a formal final session—as opposed to the clients just deciding they don't need to come back—I do use a specific closing procedure. I believe that it's useful for the clients to review where they've been, where they are now, and how they managed to progress. This reinforces their positive accomplishments and therefore their increased self-esteem and new coping skills. I review their current plans for their posttermination work on their problems in order to reinforce that and to enhance mobilization. I also use some more anticipatory planning so that they will be prepared for continuing problems. I carefully avoid taking any credit for their success, and if they offer me any, I usually respond, "Yes, you were really able to make good use of these meetings." I leave the door open for them to return in the future if needed, and I display my continuing interest and support by getting their permission for a followup phone call in a couple of months.

Mr. Jones:	I think we got a handle on it now, Doc. I don't see why we need to come here anymore.
Interviewer:	Yeah, you seem to be on top of it. This has really been a rough time for both of you.

Mr. and Mrs. Jones:	Yeah.
Interviewer:	You can look ahead and see some pretty rough things still coming up.
Mr. Jones:	Yeah, sure, but you know, like they say, the Lord will provide a way.
Interviewer:	Yeah, and you've planned things out a bit, too; like you said, right now you're worried about if Mrs. Haskins doesn't work out with the kids.
Mr. Jones:	Yeah, but you know, I called my sister, and I think she'd help a while, and that's like a backup.
Interviewer:	Uh huh. You remember, you two were pretty upset when you first came here.
Mr. Jones:	Right. My wife was all torn up over what happened and all. We just don't like to think about it now.
Interviewer:	Sure. Well, you'd really been in a spot. You know, Mrs. Jones, your mother-in-law had died [speaking to the wrong person, following Mr. Jones' lead], which left your husband pretty upset, and with no help around, and you got the bad news from your doctor.
Mrs. Jones:	And we didn't really know what it meant.
Interviewer:	Sure, and you didn't know, and your husband was so worried about you and the kids.
Mr. Jones:	I just couldn't think straight.
Interviewer:	Right—and things just built up, with your leaving, and both of you feeling bad about that, too, so there was such a row when you came back.
Mrs. Jones:	I was just so upset about the cancer, and he'd never hit me before.

Interviewer:	Yeah—really, all of this was so totally new for both of you [giving a reason for lacking an adequate coping mechanism]; you'd had no experience.
Mr. Jones:	Uh huh.
Interviewer:	I was wondering. You're both really on the tracks now, handling all the problems coming up; if you look back, what did you do that helped you, how did you get yourself back on the track?
Mr. Jones:	I don't know, things just worked out, you know.
Mrs. Jones:	Yeah, its funny, but you know, I think when we went back to the doctor, and Jim went with me.
Mr. Jones:	Yeah, that was so upsetting, I mean for my wife, you know, but at least we knew what the deal was.
Interviewer:	You knew then what was really going on, what you had to deal with.
Mr. Jones:	Right.
Interviewer:	And was it then, like that helped you start making plans, knowing what the deal was?
Mr. Jones:	Right, yeah, I talked to the neighbor then and all, and called that cancer society, and . . .
Mrs. Jones:	Yes, and you were a big help, too, doctor.
Interviewer:	Sure, sometimes it helps to have someone to talk to, to get your ideas out in the open, you know, and then you start making plans, like you two started working on these things.
Mr. Jones:	Right, that was good.
Interviewer:	You mean the talking.

Mr. Jones: Yeah, it helped me think, and then I could make plans.

Interviewer: Right.

The final step, the followup is fairly simple. I make a phone call to the clients, from three to six weeks after the last meeting, as previously arranged with them. I merely ask how things are going and check on any particular task or question that was left at termination. I listen. I may give a word of support. Basically, I try not to get very involved, but just to check in and then get out. Usually this is not difficult, as things usually are going reasonably well and the clients have better things to do than to talk to me on the phone. Occasionally someone wants to talk on, and I know then that they have some tension, that they just tend to talk, or else that I made a slight error and left them with too much dependency on me. Sometimes there are problems to be resolved, and we may make an appointment if they can't be worked out on the phone. This meeting may be to deal with a problem or with a crisis. At any rate, because of the timing, I know it's not the same crisis as before.

The point of this followup call is to extend the support beyond termination while the clients are still working out their problems and to keep some pressure on them to continue working, since they know I will call to ask. The call also lets them know that the door is open if needed for future problems, thus more firmly establishing me as a piece of their network.

The second part of closing is to write a brief summary of the case, indicating the analysis of the problem and the steps taken. This is important because my memory is poor, and these clients may call again. I believe that this step would be especially important in an agency where turnover tends to be high and someone else may get a case the next time around. The third part of closing evolves nicely from the second. Since I have to write a summary, I have to stop and think. I try to review the development of the case to increase my understanding, and I particularly think about what went well, what didn't, and why. This reflection increases my learning markedly. I make a formal commitment to myself to do this with each case. Otherwise by the time of closing I'll be caught up with new families with new problems, and this learning opportunity will slip by.

An important aspect of crisis intervention is the process of referral. Referral is used as a part of establishing a network and as a part of mobilizing. It can also be a task, and at times it is the primary aspect of the intervention. If the initial phone call makes the situation clear, and if referral is likely to be effective, then it can be handled simply over the phone: "I believe you can get some help with that at social services. That's in the white pages under Baltimore County. Will you call them and check it out? You can ask for the foster care program. And call me back if there are any problems." In this way I leave the door open, am still involved, and am providing some support and some mobilizing pressure until the contact is actually made.

Most crisis cases, though, require meeting with the clients and evaluating the situation before referral can be made. The referral may be made in order to obtain a service that will be ancillary to the crisis intervention process or that will be part of the followup work after that process. The referral may even be the crux of the intervention. The referral should arise from and during the exploring and evaluating process. The clients should be clear about to what they are being referred and for what purpose. It should make sense to them. The clients will need to be mobilized to carry out the referral, and support and followup should be built into the process. Thus, the referral arises naturally out of the crisis intervention process and becomes a task to be handled just like other tasks.

It is important that a referral be handled well so that the clients don't feel sloughed off, rejected, and bereft of support, and so they don't "fall through the cracks" and get lost during the referral process. I may make some phone calls to find out about the resource or ask the clients to do this and report back to me. I try to be sure that the clients know what we are trying to accomplish and what to expect. Anticipatory planning is useful here. Then I work with the resource and/or the clients to ensure that they connect with the services that we have decided are indicated. This lesson I learned well when I once sent a rather confused lady to an agency to see if she was eligible for temporary babysitting services. Her husband happened to take her to the agency, and they briefly wound up receiving some inappropriate marital counseling—and no babysitting.

If the referral actually transfers the case to another worker, then support and followup with the clients are important. I may schedule another session after the referral contact is to be made or at least schedule a followup phone call. This helps ensure that the clients will go, provides continuing support to bridge the transition, and keeps the intervention process going in case the referral doesn't work out.

Making a referral effectively takes a good bit of time and effort. A referral is not merely a simple way to close a case. Aside from having a responsibility to the clients, I feel that after I've spent the time and effort to do an evaluation, I do not want to have it wasted by skimping on making the referral.

Chapter Eight

Obstacles, Problems, and Special Issues

The major obstacles to success-
ful crisis intervention can be divided into four areas: the
worker's feelings, the worker's technique, the clients, and the
situation.

In doing this work, I do not try to control my feelings;
rather, I try to be aware of them, to accept them, and, to some
extent, to understand why I am having them. When I can do
so, I am in a much better position to control my behavior; that
is, my feelings will not inadvertently influence my behavior,
for example, subtly chasing away a client who provokes angry
or erotic feelings. Also, if I can be clear that my feelings are
arising from the interaction with the client rather than from
some unrelated inner source, then they can be useful signals.
For example, I find that a certain teary-eyed feeling alerts me
that the client is depressed, even though he may appear angry
or perhaps unemotional at the moment. If I begin to feel very
frustrated for no apparent reason, I begin to look more closely

at what's going on between myself and the clients. Sometimes I find that without being aware of it, I've been wanting them to react in a certain way and they haven't, or perhaps I've been reacting to a subtle effort of the client to manipulate me.

Sometimes being aware of feelings and their cause and accepting them may not change the feelings or prevent them from being a problem. The most troublesome feelings tend to be anger, depression, inadequacy, and helplessness. There are several ways to deal with such feelings. First is sharing. It can be extremely helpful to discuss a case with a supervisor or a colleague, including a discussion of my own feelings. Frequently I get very helpful comments from someone who has more distance from the case. Ventilating the feelings is helpful. Sometimes just organizing the case in order to discuss it helps to understand it better, to get new ideas, and not infrequently to change the troublesome feelings.

On very rare occasions, as a last resort, I will bring up the feelings with the clients:

"Mr. Jones, I know you're concerned about this, and I'm concerned about it, too, but I have to tell you, in spite of everything I've said, you keep interrupting your wife every time she opens her mouth, and I find it's annoying me so much I'm having trouble listening to you."

"Gee, you know, I can see how bad you're all feeling, and none of the ideas we've come up with really seem to go anywhere or seem to fit in for you, and you know, I'm starting to feel almost hopeless about the whole thing myself."

This latter intervention can be a useful paradoxical maneuver—I've had clients who have been shooting down every idea or comment I've made suddenly become very solicitous and sympathetic ("Aw, it's not *that* bad, Doc.") and begin to make their own suggestions. At any rate, sharing feelings with the client sometimes helps me to deal with them, but I do this rarely and do not generally advocate it.

There is a specific technique that is helpful when I begin to get too angry at parents for their treatment of their child: I shift over to asking the parents about their own childhoods. Generally the information I receive does a great deal to alleviate my anger—which sometimes is transformed into admiration that the parents are doing as well as they are—and then I can shift back to the work.

Often beginning crisis intervention workers feel intimidated by clients, especially if under attack for some presumed inadequacy. The simplest way to deal with this is honesty (up to a point), a little active listening, and avoiding defensive reactions:

"Mr. Jones, you're right, I have no children, and as you may have guessed, I'm not even married. I've had some special training that I find useful in working with people, but there is no way that I can really know what it's like for you trying to deal with these problems. The best I can do is to try to listen, and as you explain it, I'll see how much I can understand. You're probably worried that I may not be able to help you, and of course, we don't know yet. Maybe if you'll tell me more about this we can see how it goes."

The general formula applies whether the worker is too Jewish or not Jewish enough, too old or not old enough, too black or not black enough, or any of the myriad shortcomings that an uneasy, hostile, and understandably defensive client can bring up. It helps if the worker can remember that the client is speaking from his own discomfort rather than from any real awareness of the worker's inadequacies and that an inability to help a particular client will be a much greater loss for the client than for the worker.

A frequently recurring problem that often underlies troublesome feelings is a sense of omnipotence. This results from an exaggerated self-image—an image of the all-knowing, all-caring mental health worker who can solve all problems for the poor, helpless clients and who knows exactly how they should live their lives; this "expert" sets only large goals, and succeeds with every case. This problem occurs when I'm frustrated because I can't get the clients to do what I want—I've fallen into the trap of thinking that they *should* do what I want. One warning signal of this problem is increasing tension between myself and a client. Then I may note that I am, by persuasion, coercion, or logical argument, trying to get him to do something he doesn't want to do. I am starting to fall into a power struggle. When this occurs in this work, I automatically lose—puncturing the sense of omnipotence and leading to anger, frustration, and depression.

The omnipotence problem also underlies a feeling of excessive responsibility for the clients—not that I *want* to help them, but that I *should* and I *must* help them. Then I feel it's up to me; I take responsibility away from them, and this attitude actually impedes the work. I begin to feel angry, frustrated, helpless, and ultimately depressed. I have to remember that there are people I cannot help, and situations that I cannot resolve or change, certainly not without the clients' efforts. When I realize that once again I've slipped into the omnipotence fantasy, the troublesome feelings usually stop interfering. Then I can return to a concerned state with a problem-solving attitude and with a more detached sense of scientific interest, a position from which I have more chance of being effective.

The second major obstacle to success in crisis intervention arises from faulty technique, most often from a failure to properly utilize the described approach. Most frequently, I inadvertently fall into doing *therapy* when I am fully intending to do crisis intervention. I find myself dealing with defenses and chasing after feelings, which is a very beguiling temptation; or I find myself doing some very specific work to improve communication within a family, as though improved communication alone would resolve the crisis. The simple solution to this problem is to recognize what's happening, stop it, and return to doing crisis intervention.

On other occasions the work may not go well, and reflection will reveal a failure to define goals or to develop a plan. Or I may realize that I have been doing the crisis intervention poorly, perhaps with a lack of specificity. I may not have defined The Problem well, or I may have come up with an unworkable definition or one that the clients can't accept.

Another problem arises from failure to assess the possibilities accurately—there are cases in which the demands of the case exceed the capacities of the technique and of the worker. Omnipotence problems may have to be overcome in order to recognize this. The procedure then may be to say "I can't help" to the clients. This occasionally works as a paradox and perhaps improves the process. Otherwise, it may be possible to make a referral, but the worker may not have the leverage to do so at that point, and there may be no good reason to believe that someone else might do any better. Also, a referral may raise false hopes in the clients, leading to another morale-lowering failure for them. When the impossibility of a case is recognized and accepted, and if the clients haven't quit, it can be useful to shift to a supportive stance. In such cases I merely try to be with the clients as they go through the crisis, waiting to see how it comes out and if any opportunities for useful work arise later; I am reassured by the knowledge that the crisis is time limited. Sometimes the modest process of offering support and listening is a worthwhile endeavor.

Another frequent technical problem is overinvolvement, becoming too personally involved with the clients and their lives. One can be warm, friendly, concerned, and fairly open with clients while still maintaining a professional stance. One can even cry with a client on occasion. But there is a point at which their pain becomes my pain, and their problem my problem. At this point my professional stance is lost; without that most useful tool, my ability to be helpful is markedly diminished if not lost altogether. One common example of this occurs when I develop great sympathy for a child. Often the child seems to be a victim of inept parents whose mistreatment has warped the child's personality. This may be an accurate assessment, but it omits any understanding of what it may be like trying to live with the resultant little bastard.

Of course, the solution to this particular problem of technique is simpler to state than to achieve: The worker should maintain a professional position with his clients, without judging them, taking undue responsibility for them, or otherwise becoming overly involved. By being continually alert and self-scrutinizing, this can be done.

Another common failure of technique is making a hasty referral. Often a referral is made without assessing the problem, without knowing the resource, without eliciting the client's ideas and perceiving his feelings about the referral, and without maintaining continuing support. Such referrals are quick and easy, but frequently a total waste of time and effort for all concerned.

Certain characteristics of the clients can present obstacles beyond the ordinary difficulties of dealing with people's fear, negativism, or apathy. Sometimes, perhaps partly by neglecting to consider all the criteria, the worker can be misled by a pseudocrisis, of which there are two main types. The first occurs when someone generates a great deal of dramatic emotional turmoil, primarily for manipulative purposes—for example, to regain or to punish a lost lover or escape the legal consequences of an act. Such manipulative behavior may represent secondary coping efforts or a primary coping style. Unfortunately, some of these histrionic outbursts do reflect crises, just as suicide gestures sometimes turn out to be fatal. Usually, though, if the worker avoids being sucked into the emotionality and makes his own assessment and definition of the situation, he will note the histrionic features and understand the manipulative aspects of the behavior. Then he can provide some support, continue to sort things out calmly, and let a bit of time pass—thus obtaining some calmness, some clarity, and a diagnosis of pseudocrisis. In such cases, if the worker can figure out a maneuver that will allow the client to leave without backing down and losing face, the situation will frequently resolve itself. Otherwise, the worker may simply offer his impression and maybe therapy, perhaps offering a followup appointment, which in all likelihood will not be kept.

The second type of pseudocrisis occurs among clients for whom crisis is a way of life, clients who are continually besieging friends, relatives, and helping facilities with emergencies. In such cases there is no real crisis, since this is the equilibrium state.

Both types of pseudocrisis are quite difficult to deal with. Both types *may* be situations for which help is needed and appropriate. Crisis intervention may be a way to begin, and it may be helpful in clarifying the situation. However, this approach alone will be insufficient, and it would be a technical error to continue with it rather than to use it for shifting to some other type of intervention.

Some degree of dependency is natural in anyone who is in a crisis. However, for some people extreme dependency is a normal way of life. This presents severe obstacles to crisis intervention work with them. Their basic approach is "I'm lying here on these railroad tracks; we both know the train is coming; what are *you* going to do about it?" When this problem of extreme dependency arises in a case, the worker should make sure that he is not in some way fostering the dependency. This can occur by offering either insufficient or excessive empathic support, by doing things for the client that he could do for himself, and by expecting too much at once from a client rather than thinking in terms of small steps. If the worker determines that he has not been fostering the dependency, then the state may well be chronic and fixed. Crisis intervention may not be of much help.

Sometimes in such a situation I will try moving to an even more passive position, offering primarily sympathetic support and waiting to see what happens ("Gee, that really is terrible, no wonder you feel terrible; it looks like there's just nothing that can be done about it. You must have a good bit of strength from somewhere to have been able to endure this."). This is a power play on my part that has not been highly successful. Usually I eventually find myself reluctantly and cautiously doing more for the dependent client. Surprisingly, this sometimes turns out to be of some help: The client takes hold, and the situation improves. Usually, though, the situation does not work out, increasing demands are made upon me, and the process generally deteriorates. The crisis will be resolved but in mutual frustration and at a lower level of functioning than I desired. It is difficult to resist the pulls of the clients, and one can feel almost forced to do unwarranted things that are unhelpful over the long range ("My baby here has not eaten today and I have no food for tomorrow" implying that I can't seek or accept a job, or call my relatives, or fill out the forms for welfare).* Helplessness can be an exceedingly powerful position.

Other personality styles can create obstacles. An example is the "yes, but" game player, described by Eric Berne in *Games People Play*. This client continually seeks advice but responds to each offering with "Yes, but that won't work because . . . ." The worker can wrack his brains to come up with an effective solution to the problem, which the client so skillfully presents, but to no avail; there is always a better "yes, but."

Client:	The roof leaks, and when it rains the baby's bed gets wet and I'm afraid he'll get sick.
Interviewer:	[unable to resist the bait] Why don't you move the baby's bed?
Client:	Yes, but he cries all night if his bed isn't by the window.
Interviewer:	Why not find another window where it doesn't leak?
Client:	Yes, but I want the baby in our room, and that's the only window.
Interviewer:	Could you get the roof fixed?
Client:	Yes, but that costs too much.
Interviewer:	Could your husband do it?
Client:	Yes, but he doesn't know how.

Once the worker recognizes the game, it usually isn't too difficult to get out of it, although the client may be skillful enough to seduce the worker into just one or two more suggestions. These clients will still be difficult to deal with, though, as they will tend to "yes, but" tasks, appointment times, discussions, and so on.

The worker first must recognize and get out of the

*E. Berne, *Games People Play* (New York: Grove Press, 1964).

game. Then he can try confrontation or paradox, though neither promises great success.

Confrontation

Interviewer: I believe you're better at finding reasons that suggestions won't work than I am at coming up with suggestions. I'll bet you a quarter that the next three suggestions I make you can shoot down immediately.

Client: Yes, but how will that help me with this problem?

Paradox

Interviewer: [muttering to self] No, that won't work. Maybe—oh, no, it won't. [To client] I just had some ideas, but I can see they won't work.

Client: What are they? What won't work?

Interviewer: Oh, for a minute I thought you might ask your husband to fix the roof, but I'm sure that wouldn't work.

Client: Well, I don't know, maybe he could.

However, the more likely reply in the latter example is the following:

Client: Yes, but he wouldn't do it.

Interviewer: Yes, I know, that's what I thought, too. You know, I've just realized, you've really thought this through very carefully, you've considered all the angles; if there were anything to do you'd have thought of it by now. It must really be that there's nothing you can do about this.

These maneuvers may very well not work either, but the worker must steadfastly refrain from making further suggestions. If the client does begin to come up with ideas of his own, the worker should withhold positiveness and react with dubious pessimism, or else the ideas will then become his and the client will "yes, but" them.

Sometimes the situation creates the obstacle. Obstacles may arise from working with a bureaucratic system, for example, the legal system or the school system. Some systems do not really seem to be set up to be of maximal assistance to people. One needs experience and skills in working with, in, through, around, and on rare occasion, against systems. In crisis intervention work, it is most helpful to build up a knowledge of community resources, details of their workings, and a working acquaintance with strategic people within the systems.

When the worker is stopped by an obstacle in the situation, one good move is to redefine goals. Another is to expand the network further. Beyond that I can only comment that patience, flexibility, and ingenuity are nice assets to have, if one could choose to have them.

Finally, while there are many types of obstacles, there is also a tendency to underestimate the real value of active listening and of just being there, which sometimes is all a worker can do—and which sometimes is enough.

Special Problems

There are a number of specific problems that the crisis intervention worker, and indeed, anyone in the helping professions, will run into. Some of these problems are common, some rare, but they are special because they are difficult to handle, carry important consequences, and require particular management beyond the basic approach already described. Fortunately, not all of them arise frequently, but it is imperative that the worker be prepared to deal with any of them.

Depression. A relatively mild depression can be a result or a component of a crisis process. It usually will not require special attention beyond applying the basic crisis intervention approach. The discussion here applies to severe depressions and situations where the depression itself is the central point of the crisis situation. The more severe and central the depression, the more the worker will need to utilize the specialized approach described here; the less severe and central, the more the worker should employ the routine crisis intervention approach, merely blending in some modifications.

Depression is a medical condition with biochemical changes. The typical symptoms are many and varied: insomnia (especially early morning awakening); loss of appetite; loss of sex drive; constipation; self-depreciatory attitude; depressed mood and appearance; tearfulness; fatigue; slowed speech, thoughts, and motions; diminished concentration and ability to make decisions; diminished motivation, interest, and enjoyment; preoccupation with bodily functions and with certain thoughts; and diurnal variation—depressed people frequently feel worst in the morning and better as the day progresses. These symptoms can appear in any number and combination. Some depressed patients may overeat or oversleep rather than the reverse. Some patients show agitation, tending to continuous, restless pacing, wringing their hands, bewailing their sins or their condition, uttering the same statements or questions over and over, and not sleeping. Some depressed people do not present any of these symptoms, instead developing physical symptoms for which they seek medical treatment. The true medical depression must be differentiated from a chronically depressed attitude, from a normal and appropriate grief reaction to a loss, and from a state of unhappiness due to some unpleasant reality.

Also, this discussion does not generally apply to depression in children or adolescents, whose symptoms tend to be quite different, often expressed through actions and behavior that doesn't naturally suggest depression. These children may be brought in because of school, delinquent, or other behavioral problems, with or without an accompanying crisis. A regular crisis intervention or other routine treatment approach will apply.

The true medical depression is usually best treated by a program combining medication, supportive psychotherapy, and a carefully designed activity program. Depressions commonly present as a crisis. Crisis intervention techniques are well suited to provide the supportive therapy and the activity program needed. Unless the depression is relatively mild, as measured primarily by intensity of depressed mood and of function impairment, or of brief duration, medication should be obtained under medical supervision.

It is worth noting that many physicians tend to under-treat depression, prescribing antidepressants in doses that are too small or prescribing them for too short a time, or treating with tranquilizers rather than antidepressants. A frequent side effect of the medication is a dry mouth; sometimes blurred vision, drowsiness, or anxiety also occur. These side effects can be quite unpleasant but usually dissipate within a few days or with a reduction in dosage. Unfortunately, while side effects tend to appear at once, the medication may not begin to take effect for two to sixteen days. Therefore, tranquilizers or sleeping pills may be useful at the beginning of treatment. Some patients do not respond to one antidepressant but respond quite well to another.

In some situations crisis intervention is not sufficient or appropriate, as in cases where depression is unusually severe or psychotic or where there is high suicidal risk, a lack of cooperation, or poor environmental factors. The worker's level of training and experience will dictate when the situation is beyond him, either because such conditions exist or because the depression is not responding well to treatment. Consultation or referral will be indicated. Electroshock treatment has a high success rate in depression and should be considered. Further medical evaluation may be needed to check out possible organic diseases. Psychiatric hospitalization may be necessary. With significant depression, the danger of suicide must always be borne in mind and carefully assessed. Fortunately, most depressions respond quite well to an outpatient program using medication.

In treating the depressed client, the worker may need a great deal of patience: The client may think and speak slowly, ask the same questions repeatedly, and seem to reject or ignore most of the worker's statements. At the beginning the client may not be very amenable to discussing events and history; such discussion must come gradually. At first, focus may have to be more on the symptoms and on the depression itself, which may be initially defined as The Problem.

Support, reasonable encouragement, understanding, and a positive attitude are most important. It is also important to acknowledge the client's feelings rather than trying to argue him out of them, but the worker can emphasize the transitory nature of the feelings and the positiveness of the future. This is helpful and reassuring to the client, and it greatly enhances the worker's effectiveness when the client realizes that the worker *really* understands how he feels and is not just voicing empty encouragement. The simplest way to show the client that his feelings are understood is to describe them to him:

"I know you're feeling terrible. Depression is an awful way to feel, and when you're so depressed, it feels as though it's always been this way, and will be forever. Yet, you're on a program now which will help, and you should start feeling better within a week or two. I know that it feels like it takes all your energy to make any move at all, just to lift your arm, but you're really going to be helping yourself by starting these activities. You won't feel like doing them, you won't enjoy them, not at first, but you'll be helping yourself when you force youself to do them."

It is useful to explain depression and its symptoms on an intellectual and factual basis because it helps the client understand what he is experiencing. It is useful to establish the concept of the depression as a real entity, a thing that must be dealt with. Thus each separate symptom can be discussed, explained, and then related back to the depression ("Yes, that's part of the depression, and your memory will improve when the depression gets better."). The client will frequently try to fight the depression or the symptoms ("I try so hard not to think those thoughts; tell me how I can stop them," or "If only I had energy; tell me how to have energy in the mornings."). The client should be helped to *accept* the depression ("You have those thoughts because you're depressed. They're part of your depression and you can't stop them; go ahead and let yourself think those thoughts. They'll clear up when the depression does. What you *can* do is treat your depression, help yourself get over it. I know it's hard when you don't have the energy, but if you'll make yourself get up and do these chores anyway, *then* your energy will eventually come back. If you wait for the energy first, it won't work."). I explain the vicious-cycle mechanisms—depression leads to less energy, which leads to doing less, which leads to lowered self-esteem, which leads to more depression—and I explain that it's up to the client to escape the cycle. I emphasize the triad: "It's important to come here and talk this out, and to take your medicine, and to do these chores; these are the ways you'll get over your depression." These points must be gone over repeatedly with the client, in the sessions and in the phone calls. This provides support, hope, and mobilization.

The client usually needs help to organize himself and to choose specific and reasonable goals. The prime example is the depressed housewife who is self-depreciatory and fretting because her house has gotten terribly dirty and she just can't get herself to clean it. First, explain to her that she is expecting too much of herself. If she can accept being depressed, she'll realize that right now she can't expect herself to have her normal energy or initiative—that is just part of depression. Then explain that she is doing as most depressed people do, thinking of the project as a whole rather than in steps, and even if someone wasn't depressed, it would be hard to get started on the monumental job of trying to clean an entire dirty house. Then it is time to develop a specific, organized written plan: Tuesday, dust master bedroom; Wednesday, wash kitchen floor; Thursday, wax kitchen floor; and Friday, vacuum living room.

Although the plan must address any particular issue preoccupying the client, in general it is advantageous to plan work that is somewhat physically taxing, requires little or no mental effort, is monotonous drudgery, and has concrete results that can be easily seen. Painting, sanding, and scrubbing are excellent.

It is also important to work with the client quickly on his physical appearance, which depressed people tend to let go.

Women should be encouraged to go to the beauty shop as soon as possible, for example. A normal routine should be encouraged, since some depressed people will awaken early, stay in bed half the morning, take a nap in the afternoon, and complain of insomnia that night.

As soon as the client is moving a bit, the worker should introduce something social—a brief visit, an outing, or a movie—understanding that the client will not want to do this and will not enjoy it, but that it is necessary to do.

To the extent that the client is amenable, some active listening and developing of the chain of events need to be done. This might proceed rather slowly and cautiously. Sometimes the client is quite unaware of the relationship between his symptoms and the preceding events; avoids remembering the painful events of the past, except perhaps in a ritualized bewailing; and is embarrassed by the slowness and dullness of his mental functioning. With some clients, outlining the chain of events is extremely useful; they respond quickly and rather dramatically. Other clients never seem to get to first base with this part of the work but improve nonetheless.

A typical session with a depressed client, then, will include a discussion of tasks, symptoms, medication, and the chain of events, and frequently include spending some time with family members. The family of the depressed patient is quite important. The family should have the depression, the symptoms, and the treatment program explained in an intellectual fashion, much as they are discussed with the client. The family can be helped to avoid being too critical or harsh with the client or too indulgent or pampering. The whole situation is put on a thinking, problem-solving, matter-of-fact basis. The family can be supported by acknowledging how frustrating and irritating dealing with the client is to them. The more severely depressed the client, the more essential family members are in monitoring and supporting the treatment program. They help safeguard against suicide, and they may initially need to handle the medication. They particularly can help encourage or push the client to do the tasks. On one occasion, I had to escalate the push into force, and I had the family drag a reluctant lady to visit a relative as she had agreed to do. The less severe the depression, the more the family may be present and participate in the sessions; as the depression improves, they may be involved in unfolding the chain of events. With severe depression, I see the client alone for more of the time, seeing the family members occasionally to give them explanations, guidance, and support. Especially at the beginning, the client and the family both require frequent contact, with much monitoring and support. I will initially see a significantly depressed client twice a week, and at first I may have daily phone contact.

This approach to treatment is based on an appreciation of the dynamics of depression. Often the client is suppressing a great deal of anger, frequently at the family. If anger becomes mobilized and openly expressed, at anyone, that is usually helpful. There is guilt, with a need for self-punishment that sometimes must be satisfied. There is lowered self-esteem because of these factors and the diminished functioning. There is even a certain secondary gain through the "nobleness" of deep emotional suffering and because of the way in which symptoms impose suffering on others. The physically aggressive, ignoble, irritating, constructive task of scrubbing a kitchen floor can have beneficial effects on each of these factors. In addition to tasks and mobilization, the crisis intervention approach provides the other benefits of supportive therapy—ventilation, support, and hope—and enhances the network. The therapy also provides necessary support for the program of medication, which apparently affects the biochemical basis of the symptoms and the depression directly.

With appropriate management of all three factors—medication, supportive therapy, and activities—the patient should show some improvement within a few days to a week, and definite improvement within ten days to two weeks. If not, the case should be reassessed. At that time the worker should probably refer to or consult with a psychiatrist, and a psychiatrist should consider a consultation. The leeway, of course, depends on the severity and duration of the depression, the degree of suicide risk, the reliability of the environment, the number of treatment options left, and the professional capabilities of the worker.

Depressed clients are notoriously slow to acknowledge their own improvement, but frequently it is rather apparent to the observer. It is important to comment on noticeable improvement so as to encourage and reassure the client, but this should be cautiously underplayed. Otherwise, the client will feel frightened that he is being misunderstood, that too much is expected of him, and that the support will be prematurely cut off. He will then respond by getting worse. It must also be borne in mind that at the start of improving, when the client's energy begins to return, the suicide risk *increases*. Also, people sometimes feel and appear better precisely because they have finally made up their mind to kill themselves.

Depressed clients frequently try to terminate contact too soon once they feel better. They may feel unworthy of the attention, fearful of exploration or dependency, or embarrased by the memory of their previous condition or by the need for help. I think frequently they are largely testing to see if the worker still cares about them. It is important to struggle with them about this, giving ground slowly and continuing support. Both the support and the medication should be tapered off over an extended period of time.

Suicide. Assessing and dealing with the risk of suicide is very difficult but quite essential. Some clients easily talk of killing themselves as a histrionic, emotional, and frequently manipulative procedure. It is probably best not to get caught up in dealing with such talk very intensively, since that would reinforce the behavior and increase the manipulative power and control. An appropriate response might be, "Well, of course, you can always do that if you wish, but in the meantime it might make more sense to see what can be worked out about these problems." Such a casual response or nonresponse is quite effective and useful if the worker is reasonably sure that the actual suicide risk is small.

But how can he be sure? The problem, of course, is that he can't. He can only use clinical judgment and then proceed.

The more histrionic and blatantly manipulative the suicidal comments are, the more I am inclined to treat them lightly. However, histrionic, manipulative people do sometimes presage suicide. Another move with such people is to take them quite seriously and to begin exploring psychiatric hospitalization. This frequently clarifies the superficial nature of their suicidal comments. Occasionally it clarifies their serious nature. It gets the worker off the hook ("If you're in danger of harming yourself, this work isn't appropriate; you need to be in a hospital."). With the worker off the hook and thus back in charge, and with the issue clarified, the work can proceed. The danger, of course, is that the client may just shut up and keep his suicidal urges to himself.

There are ways to help assess the suicide risk, and this must be done with any depressed client. The first and foremost principle is simply to *ask*. This can be done with some tact: "You've been feeling pretty low? How low? Have you felt so bad you've felt like harming yourself in some way? Have you been thinking of killing yourself?" Bringing up the issue of suicide does not do any harm by suggesting it to the client. Rather, the client is frequently relieved to find that he is being taken seriously and that someone appreciates how badly he feels. If he is suicidal, he generally welcomes the chance to discuss this openly.

The client's answer to such inquiry should be explored in some detail, and the worker should not be deterred by easy reassurances. If the client protests, the worker may need to be firm and give an open explanation: "Look, I know you've got these problems we'll need to work on, but first we've got to be sure of your safety. I don't think you're going to kill yourself; I certainly hope you won't, because then we wouldn't have the chance to get these problems resolved, and what you said concerned me enough that we need to check this out first."

The risk of suicide is correlated to active thoughts of suicide. If a client has a specific plan, and if he also has the means for carrying it out, the risk is quite high. The risk is higher—not lower—if the client has a history of previous attempts or gestures. The risk is higher if the patient has known anyone who committed suicide, even if the client was not personally acquainted. The risk is higher if the patient is more depressed and less histrionic, has a physical illness, or is psychotic. Also, the degree of risk is correlated with the nature of the basic problem—how frustrating, how amenable to intervention—and with the nature of the supportive network available.

It is essential to understand that almost any suicidal client is ambivalent, with some wish to die and some wish to live. Rarely does anyone kill himself without first hinting to others and without leaving the door open to possible rescue, even at the last moment. The worker must capitalize on the wish to live, encourage it, and sometimes even point it out to the client. It is as if there was a balance scale with some factors weighing for death and some for life, and it is the worker's job to help tip this scale toward life.

Discussing suicide is one of the few times I will argue with a client. I point out the irreversible nature of suicide ("I know that right now you feel hopeless, it seems everything will be black forever, but it would be a shame to kill yourself now when you're likely to feel much better two weeks from now."). I'll even point out that suicide is *always* an available option but that it's irreversible; since it leaves no options, there is nothing to lose by trying all the other options first. I may emphasize the lasting emotional harm done to children when a parent commits suicide. I will maintain close and frequent contact with the client. I will try to get help, such as consulting a colleague to see if I've missed something, to get new ideas, and to get some emotional support for myself. This is no time to work all alone.

I try to listen carefully to the client. I do not pay as much attention to the denials and reassurances ("Oh, I'd never have the guts to do it") as I do to the danger signs. When suicide seems a genuine risk, I find myself in a state of conflict— "Maybe I'm just overreacting; he said he couldn't because he's Catholic. But then, he said he knew where to get a gun." I believe this state of ambivalence reflects the client's ambivalence. If there have been some danger signals, the situation is dangerous. I then try to make a commitment about the risk, and once I have decided it is high, I do not allow myself to be dissuaded. I do not listen to further reassurances. This inflexible attitude becomes necessary, first, because there has been sufficient evidence of suicidal risk, and second, because it is so tempting to take the easier, more comfortable path ("There's no real danger, I believe him, I was just overreacting and I don't really have to go through the unpleasant, arduous, and frustrating business of trying to get him into a hospital."). Third, once I've decided, the client can easily assign me to one-half of his internal debate. Then he can only argue the more positive side. Once I take the committed position that the client is suicidal, I take a very clear position by treating him that way. If he is seriously suicidal, then hospitalization is indicated and I will try to arrange that. I try to act firmly and decisively, taking charge as much as possible. The whole therapy/crisis intervention process becomes focused entirely on this one point—I want the client to stay alive.

I will get in touch with family members. This is one of the rare times I will violate the rule of confidentiality, if necessary. If the client will not give me permission to call someone, and if I cannot find other ways to manage the situation, I will call anyway, first explaining to the client what I'm doing and why. I try to arrange that the client not leave my office alone and usually that he not even sit in the waiting room alone. If necessary, I will cancel appointments and drive him to the hospital myself. I try to send as clear and decisive a message as I can, even though I may be wrong. If I think he is suicidal, I will do whatever I can to prevent his harming himself.

This process usually works out reasonably well, and the client is hospitalized. When this does not work out, I acknowledge my limitations. I cannot prevent a suicide—no one can if a person is determined—but I will do everything in my power to prevent it. I try to work out whatever compromises I can get and continue to send a clear, unambivalent message: "OK, you won't go to the hospital. For my own protection, and to be sure we're understanding each other, I'll write out a note stating what I've recommended and your refusal, and ask you to sign. Meanwhile, I'll call your aunt, and ask her to come so we can discuss this and she can go home with you. I'll want her to stay with you at least until we can meet again."

At this point I try to involve relatives and the whole network as much as possible and to take any possible precautions. Someone should stay with the client during the acute period. Instruments of suicide should be removed from the home. This is silly, as anyone can easily find a way to kill himself, but this act demonstrates people's care and concern, makes suicide slightly more difficult, may cause a slight delay between impulse and act, and adds to the life side of the scale. Similarly, if dealing with the patient alone, I will ask him to bring to me any guns, pills, or other instruments of suicide so I can dispose of them. While I'd prefer to have the client dispose of them otherwise, this is the only way I can be sure. If I just accept his word, he might misperceive that as ambivalence on my part. At the same time I acknowledge with him that he'll have many other options, but I am doing what I can.

I believe the worker has to become very responsible in this way, or else he sends a mixed message and the client may, at least unconsciously, perceive a message that the worker doesn't really care if he kills himself. Thus, at this point I would argue against the client going home alone or even sitting alone in the waiting room. I believe it is better to err on the side of safety and in such a way that it sends a clear and very supportive message to the client, even though he may protest.

Finally, if one does this work long enough, one will lose some clients to suicide. That is a terrible experience, and it must be dealt with adequately. The case should be reviewed carefully, looking for errors of technique and judgment. It should be thoroughly explored with colleagues. Discussion with colleagues who have had similar experiences is especially helpful. The worker will have a tumultuous reaction, and only by professionally approaching the case and by using his own professional network will he be able to avoid adverse effects, both to his further work and personally, and to learn from the case so as to improve his skills and effectiveness.

Psychosis. For crisis intervention purposes, psychosis is divided into only two classes, acute and chronic. In the acute case, a major goal is to obtain necessary treatment, including medication, fairly promptly. Generally, the family will need help to deal with the situation appropriately. Sometimes sorting out both the immediate problems presented by the illness and the particular stresses that may have precipitated it will go a long way toward alleviating both the crisis and the psychosis. Simply providing support and helping to structure and organize the client's immediate life will also be of great value. The worker must listen carefully for any indications of suicidal or homicidal dangers—and may need to ask about them directly.

No one is ever completely psychotic, and no matter what the client's condition or apparent state of comprehension, the worker should show him the same courtesy and respect that any other client receives. The worker should try to be scrupulously honest. The client should be kept informed as to what is being done and what is going to be done. Explanations, discussions, and arrangements should be kept as clear and uncomplicated as possible. Brief, rational, practical explanations are preferred. Using paradox with the client is definitely not indicated.

It can be helpful to tell the acutely psychotic client that he has had a nervous breakdown—an understandable euphemism. This is frightening, but frequently the client is relieved to know what's happening or that someone else recognizes it. Sometimes, when the family seems to have been avoiding the real problem, I'll be more blunt. "Mrs. Jones, how long has your son been crazy?"

"I'm not crazy!"

"Of course you are; when did all this begin?"

It is best to deal with the client's rational statements and ideas as much as possible and to avoid paying much attention to his irrational statements or bizarre behavior. It may be indicated to try to set some limits ("Stanley, it would be more appropriate if you sat on a chair," or "Mr. Brown, those are my private books. I'd rather you left them in the shelf please."). The worker might state his disbelief of delusions, but he should not argue about them. ("Stanley, I understand you believe the FBI is after you. I cannot disprove that, but I do not believe it. There's no point in our debating it, we're both clear in our disagreement about that.").

Once a specific treatment, including medication, is obtained for the acute psychosis, it is sometimes useful to continue with the crisis intervention process. This depends on the details of the particular situation.

The above principles generally apply in dealing with chronically psychotic clients, also, but with these people obtaining treatment is usually less of an issue. Sometimes a little help with a concrete problem or a simple explanation of some misunderstanding will rather easily resolve or avert a crisis. Nonintrusive support can be very helpful. At other times more complex issues or family relationships are involved. At any rate, the basic crisis intervention model will apply in both chronic and acute cases, with the added emphasis of obtaining treatment in acute cases.

Use of Force. This should come up rarely, if ever, but there is one valuable principle regarding the handling of a violent patient. If one must use force in an emergency situation, the use of four or five strong young men who appear to know what they are doing, who can firmly tell a frightened or agitated patient what they are planning to do and then proceed to do it, has a calming effect on the patient. The actual use of force may even become unnecessary. Conversely, the attempted use of force with less overwhelming numbers or in a hesitant fashion frightens a patient more. He does not feel he's in competent hands, he is not sure of the environment's capacity to control him, and the situation may seem like a challenge that he is honor bound to accept.

Medication. The psychiatric medications are useful and dangerous. It is important to have them available in crisis intervention work, although they should be used infrequently. Tranquilizers (minor tranquilizers) can be helpful in states of real panic or extreme anxiety. They should generally be used for only brief periods—up to ten days, say, and then only if they seem necessary. Otherwise they serve as a distraction and an obstacle to the crisis intervention work—the client expects his problems to be solved by a pill. Tranquilizers are easily subject to serious and dangerous abuse.

Antipsychotics (major tranquilizers) are essential in the psychoses. Although on occasion an acute psychosis can be resolved quickly without them, the resultant risks, turmoil, and disruption are not justified.

Antidepressants are mandatory in cases of significant depression and with lesser depressions of significant duration. They should not be used for normal grief, general unhappiness, or dissatisfaction. Tranquilizers may be useful at the beginning of treatment for an anxious or agitated depression while waiting for the antidepressant to take effect.

Sleeping pills should be used only rarely and in extremely limited quantities. A sleeping pill for a night or two during overwhelming grief or at the beginning of treatment for depression can sometimes be helpful.

Medications can be misused in numerous, sometimes dangerous ways. Sometimes the minor tranquilizers or sleeping pills are prescribed in large quantities, with automatic refills, or for extended periods of time. Sometimes patients with suicidal tendencies (any serious depression) are given access to large amounts of medication. Medications are frequently switched, looking for "just the right one," often without testing any one adequately. Multiple medications are used too often, one for each symptom, rather than treating the underlying problem. The antidepressants, and sometimes the antipsychotics, are frequently prescribed in doses too low to be effective. Probably the most frequent misuse is prescribing medication when it is not medically warranted—for various forms of unhappiness, frustration, normal grief, moderate tension, and so on—when what *is* needed is listening, support, and encouraging the client to face and deal with his problems.

Alcohol. As in car wrecks, it is remarkable how often the issue of alcohol pops up in crisis intervention. To work with these problems, the following viewpoint is as valid and useful as any other that I've encountered: Alcoholism is a chronic, lifelong disease, arising from some undefined biochemical defect that produces an abnormal response to alcohol, which is characterized by the victim's extreme attraction to alcohol and his subsequent inability to handle alcohol. The victim is no more to blame for his disease than is a diabetic, and like a diabetic, the victim is responsible for effectively dealing with his disease, which otherwise will eventually destroy him.

As a chronic, lifelong disease, alcoholism is character-ized by remissions and exacerbations, and thus, by definition, the condition itself does not represent a crisis. Alcohol can lead to various emergencies—medical, homicidal, and so on—and it can lead to crisis in a family, such as the reaction to a drunken assault or to the breadwinner losing his job. Alco-holism can then provide the backdrop against which a crisis can develop, but alcoholism cannot be the crisis itself and should never be defined as The Problem, although frequently family members and others will attempt to do so. It is practi-cally impossible to work on a problem defined as "John's alcoholism" unless John himself so defines it, and even then it's difficult. In dealing with the unadmitted alcoholic, it is better to focus on the troublesome behavior that results from the drinking than to focus on the drinking itself. Then the alcoholic can shift to the issue of controlling the drinking if he wishes. Were his behavior acceptable when he was drinking (and were it not for the physical damage to himself and perhaps the financial expense), no one would be justified in complaining about the drinking itself. It may be possible to work on "the family has not yet adjusted satisfactorily to John's continuing drinking behavior." This shift of definition is not easy to make. In general, though, it is better to focus on the crisis situation and to leave the alcoholism in the background.

The life of an alcoholic's family is frequently a cycle of crises—John's alcohol-related behavior (drunken driving, assault, and missing work) gets him into trouble; the family lies, makes restitution, or bails him out in some other way and then criticizes him; John is remorseful and promises never to drink again; John doesn't drink for a while; John starts drinking again; the family nags John about drinking; John's alcohol-related behavior gets him into trouble; and so on. The crises frequently arise at this point, and John may enter the session humble and penitent. Or, the crisis may arise in other family members, who are both reacting to the drinking behavior and using it as a rationale for their own behavior. In this case, John may enter belligerently, denying that he drinks too much, or defiantly, daring anyone to try to change him. On occasion, he may enter drunk.

The worker will often be asked to decide about a diagnosis of alcoholism, usually by the suffering wife and sometimes by the drinking husband, who is probably ready to write the worker off as an adversary if he answers yes and as a two-faced weakling if he answers no. Occasionally it is helpful to the alcoholic to answer the question affirmatively, especially if asked by the alcoholic rather than the spouse. Frequently, however, the diagnosis is less than 100 percent clear, and it is not really important to the crisis intervention anyway. What *is* important is that the wife says he is and the husband says he isn't, and that is what must be dealt with.

In most cases, although the drinking behavior forms a backdrop, it is not the chronic drinking behavior that precipitates the crisis. The family is used to that; that is homeostasis. Something must have changed to make the family's usual ways of coping inadequate and to precipitate a crisis. This change is what must be determined, following the principles of crisis intervention. If it turns out that the precipitating factor was alcohol related, then the focus is not on the chronic pattern but on the precipitant. Because of John's drinking behavior, he lost his job. This has happened several times before and the family coped, but this time it happened while Grandma was in the hospital and after John had just spent the family savings as a down payment on a new car. Thus, the focus is on the money problems, the need for employment, and the absence of Grandma rather than on the drinking.

I usually try to address the drinking by planting a seed. Sometimes when an alcoholic gets into AA, he quotes what someone said to him ten years earlier as a motivating factor. There is a buildup of experiences, interventions, and treatment attempts that over a period of years eventually help the alcoholic to resolve his problem. Thus, at some point during the session, I'll probably mention AA but not as a recommendation, and I'll probably be talking to someone else when I mention it.

If the alcoholic is unusually receptive to the idea of discussing his drinking, I may go a little further. I'll speak sympathetically of how painful it is for him to see the effects of his behavior on his wife and children, his employers, and his financial and physical conditions. If that's well received, I'll mention how powerful the pull of alcohol can be, especially strong on some people, so that they'd continue drinking in spite of the results. If that's well received—a very large "if"—I may mention that some people have found AA very helpful, but that I doubt if he's ready to go that far yet. Similarly, if the wife seems motivated, or if she continues to focus on the husband's drinking, I'll mention that some people have found Al-Anon helpful. If she really pushes me about the husband's drinking, I'll eventually push her back by responding that she really should go to Al-Anon. When she asks why *she* should have to go somewhere since *he* is the one drinking, I'll reply, "Because, he's not going to change, he's never going to stop; and if it bothers you, then you're the one that's going to have to do something, he won't." With a less pushy wife, I'll play things by ear, and may use as a task her finding out about or attending Al-Anon. This will be a short-term part of the crisis intervention plan, but it might lead to long-term results. Overall, my intention is to get in the idea of AA or Al-Anon without ever saying that anyone is or is not an alcoholic. If they decide to pursue these matters, that is their decision.

On rare occasions the situation is different. If the alcoholic seems genuinely concerned about his drinking, or if the wife or family actually seem ready to force a confrontation or to make a change, then either the process moves from crisis intervention to therapy or at least very specific and immediate referrals are made as a part of the crisis intervention, which deals with the other problems. I am skeptical about these situations because usually the husband has made these promises and the wife has voiced these threats many times before—it's all part of the homeostasis.

Generally, in working with the alcoholic family in crisis, I try not to work much with the alcoholic and particularly not to depend on him much. I will support him and include him in some ways, but in my experience he will turn out to be unreliable and resistive, and if a major component of the plan hinges on his doing something, the chances are the whole thing will fail.

There is a viewpoint that by helping resolve the crisis, one is perpetuating the problem. This has some validity, since the alcoholic often becomes motivated for treatment only when faced by a crisis that threatens real, concrete, and serious losses—loss of job, wife, or driver's license. Sometimes the alcoholic becomes motivated by confrontations resulting from his behavior while drinking, without any immediate, serious threat behind them. The crisis intervention session could be used for a confrontation, arising from an exploration of issues and facts. Things could be pushed even further by arranging a plan with the alcoholic that does require the alcoholic's competent involvement. His failure could set up a confrontation to the alcoholic (if he returns) and to the family of the seriousness and tenacity of the problem. This is more therapy for the underlying alcohol problem than it is crisis intervention, and I am not optimistic about it. It is also frustrating, tricky, and somewhat dangerous. I don't use this technique; instead I try to resolve the crisis and plant seeds.

Finally, anyone doing mental health work needs to know about the signs and the danger of delirium tremens (DTs)—sometimes the alcoholic *does* stop drinking with fatal results. Delirium tremens—"the shakes"—arises during withdrawal from alcohol and consists of agitation, sleeplessness, tremors, hallucinations, confusion, and eventually convulsions. If the withdrawing alcoholic is sleeping adequately, things are probably all right; if not, or if he shows other symptoms, he needs to be under medical care immediately.

The preceding discussion has followed a stereotypical

alcoholic situation—the alcoholic husband and the suffering wife. Of course, there are many variations of the alcoholic theme, including the opposite gender pattern. Each different case must be dealt with individually, but the same concepts and approach will generally apply.

Drugs. A number of my attitudes regarding alcoholism apply to drugs. I am quite pessimistic about the possibility of stopping someone's drug abuse. I do distinguish between the crises related to adolescent experimentation, heavy drug abuse, and addiction. I am even more pessimistic about the latter two than I am about alcoholism. Frequently the approach is to help the family adjust to the continuing drug abuse. Wherever possible, I try to use the basic crisis intervention approach and not let the drug abuse become the focus or be defined as The Problem. The crisis can be resolved. Healthier functioning may develop so that the family handles the drug abuse better and the damage to various family members is lessened or so that the family operates differently, promoting or reinforcing the drug abuse less. One outcome of the intervention may be that the abuser or the family obtains treatment. I am not optimistic about the likelihood or the efficacy of such treatment, although I believe family therapy holds some promise. There may be more reasons for therapy and for optimism in the case of the adolescent whose drug abuse is not severe, and neither the intervention nor the therapy should be drug focused.

Death. The normal acute response to the death of a family member tends to follow a pattern. There may be denial, a refusal to believe it, and perhaps a period of numbness, when the survivor sits frozen or moves about mechanically. There is usually anger—at the doctor, the other driver, fate, God, or the deceased himself. There will be grief, first intense and tumultuous, followed by a longer period of less intense grieving—remembering involvement with the belongings of the lost person, feelings of sadness and nostalgia, regrets, and crying. There is also remorse ("If only I had . . ."). There may be an initial phase of idealization, with exaggerated positive memories recalled. During this longer period, the work of grieving is done and emotional ties are dissolved so that one can proceed with the business of living. The process can be subverted at any point—a person may become stuck in one phase or aspect, or he may shift into a distorted process, such as trying to avoid the grieving altogether or intense self-recrimination.

Although a person may present as a crisis because of acute grief, it is probably not a crisis, and supporting their efforts to proceed through the grieving process can help prevent a crisis. Crises occur when a person is not proceeding or has not proceeded through the normal course of grieving and must be helped to get back on the track and do the grieving work.

The same general principles of crisis intervention apply to helping a person with acute grief and the person whose grieving process has gone awry—providing support, encouragement, and listening; helping the person deal with the problem in manageable doses rather than avoiding it; reducing some of the routine burdens and pressures on the person but, after the most acute phase, expecting some functioning. Some tasks eventually need to be done at the appropriate time, such as sorting the belongings and visiting the cemetery. Basically, the person needs some guidance and support to proceed through the normal grieving process. Sometimes, as previously discussed, there may be a significant depression, and crisis intervention alone may not be sufficient.

The same principles generally apply to helping a person who is dying—helping him to face reality in manageable doses and letting his responses indicate how much he is ready to know, while using as guidelines the general principles that knowing is better than not knowing and fact preferable to fantasy.

Acute Traumatic Reactions. These reactions may occur after any significant trauma—an accident, a death, a catastrophe, or a rape—and take a variety of forms. The immediate reaction may be hysterical, trancelike, withdrawn, remarkably calm, or incoherent. The very early course may be somewhat like the process of grieving described in the discus-

sion of death—numbness and denial, rage, grief, self-recrimination, and so on. Then the long-term, typical traumatic
reaction may quickly follow—continuing anxiety, nightmares,
insomnia, compulsive mental review of the event, and guilt.

The client needs to ventilate with support and should be
provided brief factual explanations, some reassurances, and
active listening. Some medication may be initially indicated,
but it should be used sparingly if at all. The principles of
treatment thereafter generally follow those discussed in the
previous section on death, with need for continuing support,
ventilation, facing facts in manageable doses, and the gradual
resumption of normal functioning. This appropriate immediate handling is important in preventing long-term adverse
effects. If the traumatic reaction continues, psychotherapy
may be indicated.

Organic Brain Syndrome. Over time, a worker may have a
few cases where recognizing this syndrome will be a matter of
life or death. The organic brain syndrome consists of symptoms arising from such causes as drugs and other toxins, brain
infection, brain tumors, arteriosclerosis, senility, and various
other treatable and nontreatable physical disorders of the
brain. The main symptoms are the following:

1. Confusion in general, and especially confusion as to who
   people are or where one is in place or time.
2. Labile affect, with abrupt, wide mood swings, especially
   between anger and crying.
3. Deterioration of data retention, especially inability to learn
   new material or recall recent events, while memory of
   remote times is intact. There may confabulation, that is,
   making up facts to fill in for missing data.
4. Definite changes in personality.
5. Deterioration of personal habits (cleanliness and manners).
6. General deterioration of intellectual functioning (calculat-
   ing and reasoning).
7. Catastrophic reaction. This is a reaction of great anger and
   indignation when asked a simple test question, presumably
   one that the client cannot answer, such as "What year is

this?" A typical response will be "What kind of idiotic question is that? Who do you think you are to show such disrespect as to ask me a thing like that. If you intend to persist in such asinine questions, please let me know now, because I'll certainly leave!"

Any combination of these signs and symptoms in a person indicates the need for further evaluation.

School Phobia. Whenever a case of school phobia presents for treatment, I believe it should automatically be treated as a crisis. It is imperative for the child's welfare that he return to school without delay. The longer the child is out of school, the more ground he will lose both scholastically and emotionally, and the more difficult it is for him to return. Even in chronic cases, it is imperative to move fast. At the outset of treatment, momentum can be generated that will get the child into school; but if things proceed slowly, resistance increases and the momentum is lost. Both the opinions and the approach presented here are my own, although not unique to me. There are different opinions held by respected workers, but I believe strongly in this approach and find that it works.

School phobia basically consists of a child's refusal to attend school, presumably because of fears. It is most typically seen in somewhat immature girls, age six to thirteen, who may be generally fearful. The problem typically begins when the child has difficulty returning to school after being home due to a presumably legitimate illness. The child remains home, refusing to return to school or returning only intermittently. The child is anxious whenever the issue arises and has various excuses, fears, and symptoms, such as fear of violence by peers, fear of persecution by a teacher, stomachaches, headaches, or nausea. Occasionally fear is expressed for the welfare of the mother while the child is away. This last comes closest to the truth, since the problem is a neurosis directly related to the ambivalence of the family.

In the typical case, the parents pressure the child to return to school, which results in tantrums, vomiting, hysterics, and so on. The parents, who may tend to be rather

indulgent, become confused. They think the child should
return to school, but they are not sure what is wrong and don't
know how hard to push. They receive conflicting advice from
different sources. They may begin to accept the child's excuse
as valid, or they may just become more ambivalent about a
return to school. The underlying original source of ambivalence is that a family member, most often the mother, values
the child's presence and company at home, even though
recognizing her need for school.

A few questions can usually verify the above situation
and differentiate it from other conditions. Psychosis can
usually be ruled out by observing and conversing with the
child and inquiring about any bizarre behavior. In truancy,
the child does not usually remain home but is out and actively
involved with equally truant friends, and he usually tries to
hide the absence from the parents. In school refusal, a generally rebellious, delinquent, or occasionally learning-disabled
child simply refuses to attend school, with no symptoms or
excuses beyond "I don't like it" or "It's stupid." Rather than
timidly staying at home, the child tends to do as he pleases. In
withholding, a surprisingly frequent cause of "school phobia"
or "truancy," the family is actually keeping the child at home,
perhaps to take care of an invalid grandmother. For any of
these nonphobic conditions, this approach is not applicable.

Less frequently situations are more complicated and
require further exploration, more questions of the parents,
and perhaps a call to the school. If a child was actually being
persecuted by a teacher or teased by peers, this problem would
require attention but would not warrant cessation of school
attendance; however, if a child reported being directly
threatened by children with knives, that possible real danger
should be checked out. Usually, though, questioning establishes that the child has neurotic fear, perhaps related to
hearing that someone once threatened someone else with a
knife. This further checking may occasionally be necessary
before settling on the diagnosis of school phobia, although I
have never found a realistic basis for the fears.

Given any advance information about a case, I try to

have both parents, the child, and perhaps other involved people attend the session if possible. Once the diagnosis is made, which takes little time, I immediately mobilize the parents. The family and child have come for an evaluation or for treatment, and they will be caught off guard, since I intend to have the child attending school either that same day or the next day at the latest. I begin to exhibit urgency, enthusiasm, a very positive attitude, and a great deal of expertise, and I expect the family to get caught up in this process.

I explain the diagnosis and emphasize the gravity of the problem: "Your child is indeed very frightened and extremely uncomfortable. The longer she remains out of school, the more difficult it will be to return—she will be behind in her work, have lost contact with her teachers and peers, and be out of the habit of regular attendance; most of all, she will increasingly believe that her neurotic fears are realistic."

I explain that these fears arise from what is probably still a rather mild neurotic problem; because of this, the child has had to find a reasonable sounding excuse to pin the fears on. I may explain that this is the well-known process of displacement and that such displacement is a key factor in the many cases of school phobia that we professionals see so often. I further explain that if the child is not quickly returned to school, it will be even more painful for her when she returns later, and it would be cruel to let that happen and to let her fears become stronger:

"I have even seen some youngsters where things were let go too long and they eventually missed a great deal of school, missing not only the scholastic work they need but even more importantly missing out on the normal pattern of childhood with the activities and peer relationships appropriate to their age and so crucial to their emotional and social development. No parents want their child to become an emotional cripple."

By this point a great deal of parental ambivalence is resolved; I have heavily reinforced the side of them that really wants the child to attend school. I still have not tipped my hand as to my intentions, and I begin to inquire as to who is in the family and who else might be available to help, including other relatives, neighbors, friends, or anyone else. If a child is determined not to go to school, then depending on her age, sex, and strength, it may take from two to five reasonably strong adults to get her there. In addition, the involvement of others supports and strengthens parental determination and also makes it more difficult for the parents to be wishy-washy or to sabotage the process.

At this point some grasp of family dynamics is helpful although not really essential. A typical case will involve a slightly phobic mother who has few friends or interests and who is rather resentful toward the father who works long hours and perhaps travels. Thus the mother is often left alone except for the child, who she partly uses as a substitute for the father. Because of the dependency on the child as well as her general personality, the mother may find it quite difficult to be firm with the child. In such a case, it is extremely useful to have the father make whatever arrangements are necessary so that he can take the child to school. Although someone else could probably do it, the father's participation not only impresses the child but further enhances the mother's receptiveness to the process.

Once the parents are sold and resources are lined up, it is time to spring the plan. The parents, with as much physical help as is needed, are to take the child to school tomorrow (or right from this session if circumstances allow), no matter what! The only exception is if the child is truly physically ill the next morning, and she may say she is. The only way to tell is to take her temperature and watch so that she can't cheat. If the temperature is over 100° F, the child should be taken immediately to the doctor and from there to school or home as he directs. If it's between 99° and 100° F, she should be taken directly to the school nurse. Otherwise, the child should go straight to school. I haven't yet had a child able to develop appendicitis in this situation, but I'm sure it will eventually happen.

In this situation I would explain to the parents, "Now, this is not going to be easy, because your child is going to be truly terrified, and she will fight and scheme to get out of going. It is only your firmness and determination to do what's best for her that will get her there."

Here, I use anticipatory planning. I try to think of every question, obstacle, and objection the parents might raise, and I deal with them before the parents can raise them: "Now, frequently these kids are so scared they won't get dressed. What do you do? Take her in the car and take clothes with you. Usually they then dress in the car; if not, take her in her pajamas. Now sometimes they'll vomit on their clothes—it's good to take a towel so they can wipe it off. I remember one child who locked herself in the bathroom. Does your bathroom door have a lock? Do you know how to take the door off the hinges?" Sometimes, the parents can think of still another obstacle, but its impact will be slight after this process, and it can be dealt with as the others were.

An answer can be figured out to whatever objection is raised once the basic principle is grasped—this child is going to school, no matter what. Much of this must be played by ear; only if I think the child might do it will I mention the use of suicidal threats or running away. Fortunately, children do not usually go to such extremes, presumably because they are also ambivalent (they do want to go to school), and, even more important, as the child sees that her parents want her to go to school and intend to see that she does, her conflict and anxiety begin to diminish. Also, I try to insist that the child attend school and all of her classes. If necessary, I am prepared to negotiate. I would reluctantly settle for the child going to school, sitting in the counselor's office all morning, and going home. I do not initially indicate any willingness to compromise, but the ultimate goal is to break the ice, to get the child to school, and particularly to make the child sure that the parents mean it. If necessary, I will also arrange for the child to be on tranquilizers for this process and to be allowed to leave class and go to the counselor's office if she feels unduly anxious. Throughout this process, I am extremely firm yet extremely sympathetic toward the child, even exaggerating the degree of stress she feels.

"Now, Mr. and Mrs. Abbot, I'll be in touch with the

principal as soon as you leave and explain the situation to him; so if Andrea shows up for class in vomit-stained pajamas, he'll be prepared for that."

I've not yet found a child ready to face her peers in vomit-stained pajamas, but I want to be sure that the parents and the school are prepared for it and that the child knows it.

"Now, obviously, this procedure is not only going to be very difficult for Andrea, but also exceedingly trying for you. Let me tell you though, there is a time limit. You'll only have to do this a few days. Once it is perfectly clear to Andrea that you mean what you say, she'll begin going to school without all this. The very longest I have ever seen it take is ten days, and most children begin overcoming their fear after only a few. But you should have arrangements so that you can take her again later on, because she'll be likely to test you for a day or two after a little while, just to make sure you still mean it."

Usually all of this work and planning is done in the child's presence. She usually utters a few protests of "I can't," to which I respond with great sympathy. I then comment to the parents, "You can see how really uncomfortable, how frightened she is right now just at the thought of going to school. Imagine how scared she would be after staying out a month or two." I then proceed with the plan. The child may make a threat or two, which is handled in a similar fashion. Such threats also give the opportunity to discuss with the parents what they would do if the child carried out the threats. On occasion the child has stomped or fled from the interview, which is similarly dealt with, and I continue with the parents.

If the child was not present for the interview, I will have to instruct the parents on how to tell the child what they are going to do. I tell them to give the child a shortened version of the same process I've just gone through with them, and I coach them on how to deal with the likely reactions. "Yes, I understand, but still you're going" is a good line. Occasionally, I may discuss this all in some other combination of people, but the easiest and best way is to do it once with everyone together and to let the child see the parental determination while I'm there to support them. The parents will need a great deal of support and pressure. I will plan to call later the next morning to see how it went, and I will give them my number so that they can call me immediately if any unforeseen problem arises. I may even arrange to have someone on call who can rush over and provide more support, firmness, or muscle if needed.

At some point, the parents will ask, "But, what if it doesn't work?" They may even think to ask what if she goes in the front door of school and out the back (that rarely happens with school phobias). I then use my ultimate ploy, the one I fall back on if cornered with something I can't answer, and one I often try to work in somewhere anyway:

"It will work, especially if you're definite and firm, and show her you really mean it. Of course, it really doesn't always work; it works about 98 percent of the time. I've personally seen two cases where it didn't work. One of them was my fault, a mistake on my part. Nothing the parents tried worked, I don't remember exactly what happened, the girl kept jumping out the window or something. Anyway, it didn't work, and the girl had to have a more thorough evaluation, and it turned out she was crazy and I'd just plain missed it. I felt terrible. The girl had to be put in a hospital for treatment, which was what she needed, and I think she eventually did OK. Anyway, I've talked to Andrea, and it's pretty clear she's not crazy, right?

"The other case I never did figure out, but again, it just didn't work, the parents tried every day for twelve days, they really tried hard, and it just kept being a struggle. Finally, the school board had the case in court, and the judge sent the boy to the Maryland Children's Center for twenty-one days for an evaluation. They couldn't figure it out there either, but the boy went back to school after that. Everyone was surprised."

Occasionally, when I'm seeing such a case for the court, I will answer differently, although I never threaten: "Well, if it doesn't work it will just mean I'm wrong, and I wouldn't know what else to do. Probably the judge would send Andrea to the Children's Center to see what they could think of and if they could figure out why my evaluation was wrong."

Once all this is done, the next move is to arrange

therapy, counseling, or at least a therapeutic evaluation for the child. This is because the child may well have a significant emotional problem that needs treatment and at the least can use some extra support while resuming school. I usually will arrange for the school counselor to see the child at once for support until other arrangements are made. I tell the parents that the child will need treatment but that the return to school is the first, most urgent step. The treatment can then help her adjust to that. I have occasionally treated the child myself with satisfactory results, but it is easier to have someone else do it; then I can be the bad guy while the other person is sympathetic.

Everything I say to the parents is true, although I may exaggerate somewhat. If necessary, I would make up something to help get the child back to school. I try to teach the parents about school phobia, telling them anything I've mentioned here except for parental ambivalence. On that point, I assume that the parents desperately want their child to return to school but have merely been thrown by this problem that is so strange to them, and I proceed full speed ahead upon that assumption.

The success rate for school phobia has been quite high, and the children tend to do well. The crux of the issue is the parents' firmness; once that is established and made clear to the child, the process usually goes much more simply and smoothly than I have suggested to the parents. The first morning is the big hurdle.

Multiproblem Families. It is estimated that for many public agencies, departments of juvenile services, departments of social services, and so on, 15 percent of the families dealt with provide over half of the problems and use up a majority of the available time and resources. While characteristics of these families vary, there are certain consistencies. Typical multiproblem families constantly are struggling with a multitude of problems. They tend to be involved with several agencies, which are often working at cross-purposes and are unaware of each other's involvement. These families tend to have frequent crises, and to contact the agencies only during crises. Once a crisis is eased, they do not follow through with recommendations, plans, or programs. They tend to miss appointments and never to get closely involved with a worker. When they do get involved, it is usually in a hostile and dependent fashion. The majority of these families are poor. They tend to have unrealistic expectations of the worker and to be resentful of many aspects of the services offered. They seem to have endless needs, swallowing up services and sometimes workers with little visible benefit.

Such families and their crises are suitable for crisis intervention. However, crisis intervention should be only one aspect of an overall program. In the ideal program, one worker would assume long-term responsibility for the family, function as a case manager, and monitor and coordinate the involvement of other agencies.

The worker must accept the family's crisis orientation and be willing to work with them on that basis. The worker must also accept the family's chronicity and be able to appreciate small amounts of progress over long periods of time. Hopefully, over a long time the family will increasingly trust and rely on the worker, who can then be more effective with them. The worker's position is enhanced if he can function as an advocate, coordinator, and broker for the family with other agencies. It will help if the worker can schedule appointments at the family's home rather than at his office. An occasional casual home visit will also help. The worker should not try to push the family into therapy, into facing or working on basic problems, or into anything else. The worker should be available on call as a continuing resource. Eventually the family should make some progress toward health through the consistent, organized provision of appropriate assistance, through the presence of continuing support, and through identification with the model of behaviors that the worker presents—such as impulse control and problem solving. I believe the ideal worker for these cases is a grandmother, with the second choice a husky male over thirty years old.

Unfortunately, most agencies do not have the resources—time, money, personnel, or the motivation—for such an approach. Instead, they spend even more time and money in a less effective, piecemeal approach. Rapid staff turnover means that the family sees a different worker every few times they come in, and the frustration of working with such families in such a fashion contributes to the turnover problem.

When first working with a multiproblem family, it is important to focus on the immediate crisis that initiated their request for help, if they did indeed request it. This may be a point of entry so that other problems can be worked on, but the crisis must remain the primary focus. If additional problems are picked up, they should be concrete and practical in nature and limited in scope. They should not relate to emotional or dynamic issues or require changing the family structure or way of functioning. Since these families tend to be low in resources in most if not all areas, it is not wise to overtax them by adding many tasks or obligations. A simple appointment can present nearly overwhelming difficulties in coordinating the family, managing use of a telephone, missing work, arranging transportation, and general organizing.

Thus, the worker may be of assistance to the family in obtaining legal aid for Johnny in his third circuit through the juvenile court system. He might use that opportunity to get June enrolled in the adolescent pregnancy clinic program, especially if the clinic has nurses who make home visits, and even to get Grandpa checked for TB and Benny for epilepsy. However, the worker would do well to establish priorities and pursue these problems one at a time. He is liable to find, for example, that Grandpa failed to keep his chest X ray appointment because Thursday is bingo day, that the family cannot afford to pay for the medication prescribed for Benny's epilepsy, and that to become certified for free medicine involves forty cents bus fare and Benny's birth certificate, neither of which they have. The worker should not deal with Father's alcoholism or Mother's lack of a budget and wasteful buying habits. The worker should not intrude or push or become overly enthusiastic. A low-keyed approach is needed; the worker should offer services as indicated but easily accept a family's rejection of an offer. Although the family may present the crisis with a great sense of urgency, they may not actually have the desire or the resources to do too much about it, and the worker should realize that this crisis is only one of many, and there will be many more. Ideally, the worker's long-range goal should be to increase involvement with the family. To accomplish this may actually require somewhat less involvement than usual during the crisis, maintaining a somewhat matter-of-fact, distant stance, and resisting any tendency for a family's crisis to become the worker's own crisis or his own responsibility. The worker should not expect much from the family. Where the worker's situation allows it, he should employ small long-range goals and continuing case management.

Special Issues

There are several special issues of importance to the worker in crisis intervention; fortunately these are not necessarily special problems. The issues are ethics, knowledge, humor and the worker's network.

Ethics. The ethics involved in crisis intervention work are those of any professional worker. The worker's primary obligation is to the client, and many questions are resolved by asking "What would be best for the client?" This obviously involves using clinical judgment, not giving the client everything he wants. The worker is obliged to treat the client with dignity and must respect the client's right to run his own life as he chooses. The worker must receive gratification from doing his job and from his outside life; he must not use the client to gratify his voyeuristic, sexual, or sadistic impulses. The worker must carefully guard and maintain the client's confidentiality, something that is frequently and casually violated these days. The worker is obligated to do his best in each case, which means he must apply a great deal of effort and thought rather than proceeding mechanically or on the basis of feelings and intuition alone. The worker is further obliged to examine himself and his work continuously and to strive to improve his knowledge and skills constantly.

There is currently much professional debate about the ethics of paradoxical maneuvers. The purpose of these maneuvers is to influence (that is, to manipulate) the client to

behave in certain ways desired by the worker without reveal-
ing the nature or intent of the maneuver (that is, to conceal or
deceive). Yet, the underlying purpose is to benefit the client
and to provide him the assistance that he has requested,
specifically, symptom relief. Although the fundamental idea
of paradox involves manipulation and deceit, each specific
maneuver examined singly may not appear quite so manipulative or so deceitful. When using a paradoxical maneuver, I
always find at least a grain of truth in the statements; were that
not so, I doubt that I could deliver them effectively. Generally
the maneuvers focus on one aspect of the situation and ignore
others. In any form of therapy, the worker chooses what
information to share with the client and what to maintain
privately and how to phrase his statements so as to obtain the
desired effect. He subtly influences the client, even if only by
paying more attention to some topics than to others.

I only use those forms of paradox with which I feel
comfortable. I rarely if ever use paradox in therapy, where the
nature of the relationship is different. The ethical question is
a valid one with no clear-cut answer, and each worker must
reach his own decision.

Knowledge. Of course, the worker needs knowledge of
crisis intervention and must have a commitment to continued
learning. There are topics that a crisis intervention worker
should know about in more depth than is covered in this basic
book. These include alcoholism; mental health laws (particularly those governing confidentiality and commitment); normal development of children, adolescents, and adults; parenting approaches and problems; and a melange of juvenile
problems (such as hyperactivity, minimal cerebral dysfunction,
and learning disabilities). Some recommended readings (some
of which are cited in this book) are the following: R. Maxwell,
The Booze Battle (New York: Praeger, 1976); J. Haley, *Problem-
Solving Therapy* (San Francisco: Jossey-Bass, 1976); S. Minu-
chin, *Families of the Slums* (New York: Basic Books, 1967);
E. Kubler-Ross, *On Death and Dying* (New York: Macmillan,
1969); and the journals *Family Process, Adolescence,* and *Journal
of Child Psychiatry.*

Obviously many other topics can be usefully explored. More knowledge about family dynamics can be helpful if one doesn't let it become overly important in the work. Certain situations besides death, such as the birth of a premature baby (or of any child), the leaving of a last child, and retirement, are accompanied by a usual reaction course and typical problems, and knowing these are useful. Any knowledge that a mental health worker might have will be helpful, but what has been discussed plus what has been mentioned above is more than sufficient for a foundation. Thereafter, experience is the best teacher, especially if supplemented by supervision and consultation.

Humor. I find humor very useful in the crisis intervention work when used judiciously. It eases the tension and intensity of feelings, reduces the sense of threat, may enhance rapport, and helps me maintain some distance from the crisis process and the problems. Sometimes by using humor and double entendre, I can get topics discussed that otherwise might be unapproachable. Also, humor can make the meetings more fun, both for me and for the family.

Worker's Network. The worker's effectiveness is greatly enhanced by developing his own supportive network, which is partly a political process. It can be most helpful to have a personal relationship with people in various social agencies, clinics, school systems, police departments, court systems, and so on. It is even more useful if this network includes people of influence in their areas. It is useful to have working relationships with physicians who can be counted on to work cooperatively in providing good medical care, including physical examinations and prescribing psychiatric medications appropriately. One needs knowledge of and relationships with a variety of resources to which clients can be referred for psychotherapy, especially family therapy, with some assurance that the case will be well handled. Finally, and perhaps most important, the worker needs easy availability of a number of colleagues skilled in crisis intervention and mental health work who can provide support and consultation. This work cannot be adequately handled alone.

Chapter Nine

Analysis
of a Case

It is suggested that the reader use this chapter as an exercise, actually working out each analysis step on paper before reading further, proceeding just as the case worker would. The case will be presented in phases, with an indication of the analysis necessary at each point followed by a discussion of a suggested approach. Methodically going through this process should help in comprehending and clarifying the concepts that have been presented.

Phase 1

Mrs. Baker calls and says she needs help desperately. She sounds agitated and begins to sob. She says that she's been unable to sleep for the past two nights and can't even do her housework for worrying. She says she just doesn't know what to do with her fourteen-year-old son, who hasn't been listening to her and who is becoming a criminal. A question about this reveals that he was nearly arrested three days ago for stealing beer. When asked, she states that she, her husband, and the son, Bill, are living at home; her other children are gone. An appointment is set for the next day, and she agrees to try to bring Bill and her husband with her, even though she says, "I know my husband won't come."

Task 1. At this point the worker should formulate some hypotheses regarding the existence of a crisis, the nature of the problem, possible obstacles to the work, and a tentative plan for the first session.

Discussion 1. The data given suggest that Mrs. Baker is in a crisis, which is apparently related to the boy's theft. His increasing autonomy may also be a stormy and troubling process. Other family members or the family as a whole may be in crisis, but that isn't particularly suggested. Most likely, this is a problem of adolescence in the family, which may be exacerbated by Bill being the last child. He may have been spoiled and babied, making growing up particularly difficult, and he may feel driven to prove his masculinity. The father may be relatively uncommunicative and shun dealing with emotions, psychological issues, and conflict, or he may just be angry or fed up. There is at least a hint of marital tension. The whole call suggests that Mrs. Baker runs things, or at least tries to.

Various problems may arise. One is Mrs. Baker's tendency to exaggerate and label. The worker will need to use active listening to let her ventilate, while carefully controlling and plussing to prevent her from agitating or turning off either of the males or to keep her from berating one of them and getting into an argument. Relabeling the boy may help to defuse things. If discipline is far gone or if things are too hot, bargaining or role playing may be needed.

A second possible problem is Mr. Baker's negativism. It will be important to establish a positive relationship with him quickly and to keep him actively involved in the session while carefully avoiding matters or areas that he'll balk at; relabeling him may help, perhaps labeling him as a "concerned father."

The third likely problem is that the boy will be a sullen,

hostile adolescent. It will be important to be low-key with him and to avoid getting into the losing position of trying to draw him out. An indirect way to establish a positive relationship and get him somewhat involved should be sought. If he's really resistive, ignoring him and later using a few stimulating comments spoken to others might be the best bet; talking to the wrong person may be a good approach. During the ignoring, just keeping his parents off his back may help develop a relationship.

A fourth issue is to start listening early for any hints about tasks that might be enticing to Mr. Baker and to Bill. If Mrs. Baker is the only one in crisis, she may be the only one who can really be worked with.

The worker must remember that these are tentative hypotheses, and the situation may turn out to be entirely different. The data suggest that the worker may also have to guard against attempting family therapy and getting too interested in individual psychodynamics.

Phase 2

The whole family does arrive. Mr. Baker explains that he agreed to come "once, to clear up this nonsense. She makes mountains out of molehills. After all, boys will be boys." Father is thereafter relatively taciturn. Bill appears both sullen and scared but responds a bit to a direct question. Mrs. Baker is distraught. Through use of the principles of crisis intervention, the following information and impressions are obtained during the first fifteen minutes of the interview.

This marriage has never been particularly happy or close. Mr. Baker works hard in a steel mill, sometimes having to rotate shifts. He seems to fear being dominated by women and has tended to avoid involvement with the family. He likes to drink with the boys and feels entitled to do so. This has been a source of constant low-grade tension between the parents, partly because Mrs. Baker's father was an alcoholic. Mrs. Baker seems to have spent most of her married life wrapped up in her children, and doing things for them has kept her busy. The two older children, a boy and a girl, have grown up and left home, four and two years ago, respectively.

Three years ago Mr. Baker was in the hospital for a few weeks for back surgery. At that time a neighbor took Bill and his sister in while Mrs. Baker worked. Mrs. Baker's sister came and helped out each time Mrs. Baker was giving birth.

Bill plays baseball and likes mechanics. He occasionally helps his father tune the pickup. Mr. Baker sometimes attends Bill's ball games, while Mrs. Baker doesn't care to. In the past year Bill has been increasingly irritable toward his mother, which upsets her. Bill's grades have been slipping over the past year or two, and he recently brought home a failure slip in English.

Three days ago the manager of a drive-in shop caught Bill and a fifteen-year-old friend stealing a case of beer from his storeroom. Bill has no other known offenses and denies any others when his parents ask him in the interview. The manager called Bill's mother, who got quite upset. She immediately confronted Bill, who acknowledged the incident. He couldn't or wouldn't give any explanation, neither at home nor in the interview. Mrs. Baker became increasingly angry and upset, and told Bill he was grounded for two months, including from his ball games. He told her he would go anyway and that she couldn't stop him.

She became even more upset and called Mr. Baker at work. He left the job immediately, stopped at a bar for a couple of drinks ("to relax and think about the situation"), and went home. When he asked Bill why, Bill answered with a shrug. Infuriated, he beat Bill with his open hands and his belt. Mrs. Baker tried to stop him and defend the boy unsuccessfully. This is only the third time Mr. Baker has laid a hand on the boy, the last being four years ago when Bill left some of his father's tools out in the rain. Since the beating, the parents are barely speaking to each other, and Mr. Baker has been talking about moving out of the home because he's tired of all the hassles. Bill has not been speaking to either parent, although he does so minimally in the interview.

Task 2. The job at this point is to assess the situation,

using Aquilera and Messick's model to assess inadequacies, to formulate a tentative definition of the Problem, and to develop a tentative plan for handling the remainder of the session. In formulating these ideas, the worker will use both the data presented and hypotheses derived from it. These hypotheses would then be tested as the interview proceeded.

Discussion 2. Mother is in crisis; no one else is, although the family as a whole may be.

Equilibrium: tense, distant marriage; uninvolved Father drinks; Mother wrapped up with Bill. Bill's antagonism with his mother and his falling grades may be considered equilibrium also, depending on the time frame chosen.

Inadequate Perceptions:*

Mother:	1.	"I'm losing my son."
	2.	"Without a child I'm without value."
	3.	"My son is bad."
	4.	"My husband is bad."
	5.	"I'm a failure as a mother."
Bill:	1.	"My mother wants to control me."
	2.	"My mother won't let me grow up."
	3.	"My father doesn't love me anymore."
Father:	1.	"My wife wants to control me."
	2.	"My wife wants to control my son."
	3.	"I'm unable to cope with my family's problems, and I'm a poor father and a poor man."
Family:		"We are inadequate."

Inadequate network:

Mother:	1.	usually leans on kids, but two are gone and Bill is alienated
	2.	possibly too ashamed of the "criminality" to discuss it with neighbors or sister

---

*Some of these perceptions are inadequate not in the sense of being wholly inaccurate but in being one-sided, distorted, and interfering with functioning. For example, Bill's perception that Mother wants to control him and not let him grow up may be somewhat accurate, although she's probably ambivalent. However, she can't "not let" him grow up—that's up to him.

            3. few outside contacts

Bill: 1. too embarrassed of "criminality" and/or beating to discuss it with anyone helpful, such as older brother or peers

            2. possibly no nondelinquent friends

            3. possibly antagonistic to adult authority and without nonfamily adults to rely on

            4. possibly receiving no support for growing up (a more chronic problem)

Father: 1. only get criticism from wife

            2. may rely on friends in bar, who may give poor advice

Family: 1. all currently alienated from each other, so mutual support is lacking during crisis

            2. embarrassment possibly cutting off outside sources

Inadequate coping mechanisms.*

Mother: 1. leaning on Bill now impossible

            2. possibly no previous experience in coping with an uncooperative adolescent

            3. secondary coping mechanism of calling Father failed

Bill: 1. uses passive resistance and acting out for autonomy problem, which worsen situation

            2. no previous experience being an adolescent

            3. no experience in dealing with physical confrontation with Father as an adolescent

Father: 1. use of avoidance, withdrawal, and letting Mother handle problem fails since Mother cannot do so

            2. possibly no experience dealing with problems and discipline of an adolescent

            3. use of force more effective with a younger child but leads to more problems with an adolescent and to more conflict with Mother

* Depending on the assessment of the crisis and the definition of The Problem, some of these inadequacies will apply to the present crisis situation and others to chronic underlying problems.

Family: 1. possibly no experience with criminal acts,
            school problems, or adolescent turmoil
         2. no experience with change in family struc-
            ture resulting from last child growing up

There are several candidates for The Problem:

1. "The family hasn't yet adjusted to the recent battle among themselves." This definition is better than focusing on the beating, which is still too hot and which would inflame Bill and make Father look bad. However, this definition doesn't cover enough ground, especially because it leaves out the theft, an emotional issue that may or may not have been settled by the beating.
2. "The family hasn't yet resolved the issue of the theft." This focuses too much on Bill but can easily include the beating as one part of the process.
3. "The family, including Bill, has not yet adjusted to Bill's adolescence." This definition is too broad and general, and it doesn't fit the family's initial focus on the beating and the theft. It could be introduced later on to deepen the focus after the more immediate issue is dealt with and defused. However, it is too hard to *do* anything about, gets too close to therapy, and is exactly the kind of idea that will turn off Father and probably Bill.
4. "The family has not yet adjusted to the growing up and separation of the last child." The same comments apply as in candidate 3. In addition, this is probably too hot to handle. The idea should be casually mentioned in passing at some later point.

I plan to begin where the mother did, which seems, superficially at least, to be the theft. As I learn more about the theft and the family's reactions to it and begin to formulate the chain of events, I should be able to gradually shift the focus onto the beating and their reactions to that. The theft does seem to be the primary precipitant for most of this crisis, although the situation might have been worked out without a crisis were it not for the secondary coping effort of the beating, which served as a secondary precipitant. I am defining The Problem to myself and to the family largely by implication. It is "In the midst of struggling with the difficult process of a last child's adolescence, the family was faced with an event that no one really knew how to deal with—a theft—and as each tried to handle it, their efforts seemed to backfire, leading to an incident—the beating—which no one wanted and which has temporarily left them upset and perhaps even a little confused." Of course, I will probably never make such a statement in its totality to them, but the statement will evolve out of my questions, comments, and how we piece the chain of events together. This formulation seems workable, includes some useful seeds about the deeper problems, is palatable to the family, and also happens to be fairly accurate.

Although Mrs. Baker initially called about the theft, the beating is the critical issue and must be dealt with before the family can work together and be mobilized. It is a very hot issue, and I don't want to start with it or make it the focus. I intend to work out a chain of events, starting with the background to the theft, using the theft as the central precipitant, and downplaying the beating as a reaction to the theft. In this way I hope to work out and defuse the beating issue, without any angry eruptions, partly by not letting it become the center of the discussion and partly by using the various techniques, especially keeping in charge, plussing, and relabeling, and by using the problem-solving attitude.

I see the father as the key to the situation. He doesn't want to be involved, feels very threatened by the interview and by the family situation, and feels very inadequate and very guilty. Unless handled properly, he is liable to sabotage this session and the rest of the work, and Bill and Mrs. Baker will use him as a convenient scapegoat. My immediate plan then is to first enhance Mr. Baker's self-esteem and to avoid any kind of power struggle with him. I plan to treat him with great respect and to label him as the "hard worker" and the "concerned father." This will be done in the course of the chain of events, as well as during the assessment of the situation using Aquilera and Messick's model:

"So, let's see, Mr. Baker, you'd already put in four hours

in front of this blazing furnace, and you're tired and hot, and then you get the phone call. Now, when you get this call, you don't put your wife off, or dump it back in her lap; you ask your foreman and you head for home. Now you hadn't had any experience with anything like this before, and naturally, you weren't sure what you'd do. You stopped in the bar to think things out a bit before just jumping into the middle of things?

"So, Mrs. Baker, you really didn't know what to do then, so naturally you called your husband. Now I gather you don't do that often, call him at his work like that? So, you know he's working hard there, and can't just drop the job for things easily, and you wouldn't have called him if you hadn't thought it was important, right? So, Mr. Baker, when your wife called you at work, you knew it must be important, right? Of course, Mrs. Baker, if you'd known what was going to happen, how all this would turn out now, you wouldn't have called your husband, you didn't want all this, but you didn't know what to do.

"So, Bill, here's your father coming home, and more why questions; if you're like most people I meet, you don't really know the answer to those why questions, and you also don't know what your father's gonna do. And Mr. Baker, you get home all tired and worried, and of course, you aren't sure what to do, nobody knows how to handle these things and you hadn't been in this before, so I guess the whole thing blows up, which isn't what you wanted. You probably wind up feeling you're not much of a father, 'cause if you're like a lot of people, you expect yourself to somehow automatically know what to do with these problems. And of course Bill here, he's mad and scared and doesn't understand what's behind this beating, he was maybe even thinking his father doesn't love him. So everybody winds up pretty unhappy with the way things have gone about all this."

Mrs. Baker has been relabeled from the critical, controlling wife to the mother who doesn't know what to do, Mr. Baker from the drinking beater to the hard-working, concerned father, and Bill from the negativistic thief or the

pathetic beating victim to the scared boy who's being asked
questions he can't answer and who is misguidedly questioning
his father's love—which thereby relabels Mr. Baker as an
important and loving father. The ideas that Mr. Baker should
know what to do and that maybe he doesn't love Bill have been
openly expressed and then labeled an unrealistic. The whole
sequence of events has been seen as a logical consequence of
the actions of concerned people with good intentions. The
parents have even been unobtrusively instructed to quit asking
why questions. Working out the chain this way will help the
family maintain some emotional distance from the data and
will keep me in charge as I talk to each of them separately, do
a lot of the talking myself, and keep them from talking to each
other at this still hot stage of things.

The sticky point here is Mr. Baker's threat to leave
home. I assume that this represents an angry, frustrated,
self-pitying, and somewhat manipulative emotional expression, and I plan largely to ignore it and proceed on the
assumption that he'll be at home. I would like to get this chain
of events worked out and the beating defused before getting
into his possible leaving, and then I hope it won't come up. If
it does seem more pressing, I may include it in the comments
in passing ("So somebody could see how you might even think
about leaving home at that point; and then, next you start
wondering why Bill . . ."). This would be a test balloon to see
how or if he'd respond, to gauge his intent; it also gives him
the out that the thought of leaving home was merely a passing
emotional response to the heat of things. If his leaving does
get pushed, I will carefully avoid taking a position on it and
even try to plus it ("So, you're thinking if you're not home for
a while that might give things a chance to cool off more? Is it
seeming to you that things can get thought out more that way
than if you're all together right now?").

I definitely would not try to dissuade him from leaving.
If he really seems to be going, I will handle this rationally and
unemotionally as a part of the planning process ("Now, do you
know yet where you'll be staying?" or "Would you like me to
call you then after we find out about Bill's school reports?"). I

will assume his continuing interest and eventual return home. Handling it this way reduces everyone's emotionality and undermines the manipulative aspect, which may lower the chance that he'll go. It is important to help him have a way to stay home, to avoid setting things up so he'll lose face if he doesn't go. Arguing or actively opposing his leaving would do just that—he would have to go to demonstrate that he runs his own life. Of course, I hope that he's not just using the situation as an excuse to move in with his girl friend. If he is, presumably there'll be ongoing crisis work with Mrs. Baker.

If the family has gone along with me through the chain of events, and if the leaving issue hasn't blown up, then we may have eliminated some of the difficulties caused by the beating and cleared the field so that we can work on problems. I will then begin to shift to the idea of *needs*. I may begin like this: "You know, I've been wondering about this school business. Bill, do you like school? . . . Have you always hated school, or just recently? . . . What's the hardest thing for you in school?" Of course, if Bill isn't willing to discuss all this with me, I can ask the same questions of the parents. I am going to have Bill relabeled as a baseball player and as a boy who may have some learning problems and who *needs* some investigation of this possibility. Then I give a task, which is to have the parents (as much as the father seems willing) become involved with the school about the matter. I may even try to stir up a little antagonism toward the school, a little crusading spirit, to increase their motivation, to give them an extra family outlet for their anger, and to help them get themselves out of the inadequate villain role. Turning their attention to Bill's need for a scholastic evaluation will give them something to do, so they can be assertive and not feel helpless; and it will give them a task that will show they're doing a good job of being parents. Bill will see them going to bat for him, which may turn up a source of positive support and modeling for him—such as a school counselor, psychologist, or assistant principal. He may get some extra scholastic help and positive attention at school, and the process may even turn up a learning problem that needs attention.

As I go through this scholastic-need move with Bill, I will also begin to introduce the needs of the parents, because I don't want them to feel slighted in favor of Bill: "Mrs. Baker, do you know any of the parents whose kids have had grade trouble in school this year? Have you had a chance to talk to someone like the vice principal or the school counselor yet? I don't know if you've been kind of carrying your worries around, maybe keeping them to yourself?" She needs support.

Mr. Baker, the hard worker, needs some rest and peace and quiet: "Mr. Baker, you must be generally exhausted by the time you get home, and I bet it's pretty hard to get the foreman to let you off except in a real emergency? And your days off must really be pretty precious to you. How did you manage to make it today?"

Mother's and Father's needs are noted and at the same time tied into their task: "Mr. Baker, look, it's obvious you're concerned about Bill, but I don't see how you're gonna manage working so hard and getting involved in this school business, too." Father may jump in and say he damn well will manage—if the school isn't doing right by Bill, he will be there to see about it. He may eventually persuade me, but not easily ("But look, first, you're going to be tired, and what if they can't see you on an afternoon when you're off?"). I don't want Father to get all fired up to go, lose his enthusiasm after he leaves my office, and either not go or go resentfully. However, he probably won't jump in like this, and he probably won't be going.

Once we agree that it's unreasonable to expect him to go, then I'll probably try to get him involved: "Look, I'll be asking Mrs. Baker how her meeting went, but I'll certainly want to hear your impression of it. Now, I don't want to disturb your rest and relaxation, or interrupt you if you're busy. When's a good time I could call you after she's had a chance to tell you about the meeting?" Here I'm setting up another task—they're to discuss the meeting.

I will use the same approach in dealing with the question of Father attending these sessions. I assume that he won't come back no matter what I do, and that if by some chance I could coerce him into coming, I would regret it. He *may* argue me down ("Well, all right, but look, if you're really too tired that afternoon, you can still change your mind."). That would be the only useful way in which he might come, and this approach maximizes the possibility; but he probably won't. I would certainly like him to come, but I'm accepting the reality. By not trying to persuade a reluctant man to do something, I keep in control, keep a positive alliance with him, and don't damage his image as a father and a man, all of which is probably more important than his coming anyway. With this approach we can likely keep a phone contact going, and he won't be resentfully sabotaging the work. This is a major issue, because whether he comes or not, if he sees me as putting him down or threatening him, he will defeat me.

So: Bill the baseball player needs a scholastic evaluation; Mr. Baker the hard worker and concerned father needs some rest, peace, and quiet; and Mrs. Baker the concerned mother needs someone to talk things over with and someone to call in an emergency. As tasks these concerned parents will check into Bill's needs at school: Mrs. Baker will call to see if she can make an appointment; the Bakers will discuss this call and the appointment if it occurs; and Mr. Baker will then tell me his impression of the situation. We will also agree that if any emergencies arise between now and our next meeting, Mrs. Baker will call me before calling her husband. If she can't reach me within a half hour, then she will call him if necessary, but it is preferable not to call him at work.

I have not involved Bill in any tasks. I have considered several things: having him come in to further evaluate him and to discuss with him the results of the school appointment, letting him wash his father's pickup to show his remorse for all this trouble, and arranging things so that he can have more time with his father or his coach. However, I'm short of time in the session, I'm getting along fairly well with him and don't want to push my luck, and I think the crisis will be resolved anyway, probably with some benefits to him. In addition, he's not in crisis. Thus I let him be indirectly involved through the school appointment, which directly concerns him.

My goals for this first session, beyond the routine goals, (Steps 1 through 5) have been (1) to defuse the acute animosity among the family members, (2) to establish a positive relationship with Mr. Baker in particular, (3) to get Mr. and Mrs. Baker cooperatively involved in a parental task, thus improving their self-images, reducing marital animosity, and providing Bill with a sense of parental support, and (4) to expand Mrs. Baker's network.

Task 3. The worker, by the end of this first session, should have formulated plans for the next session and for the whole course of the intervention.

Discussion 3. I have established the following overall goals for resolving this crisis: increasing parents' self-esteem, diminishing general animosity, increasing the support available to Mrs. Baker and Bill, and diminishing Mrs. Baker's pressure on Mr. Baker and Bill. Important subgoals, then, are relabeling people and situations, increased parental functioning, and extending Mrs. Baker's network and interests outside the family.

My plans for the second session are primarily to increase Mrs. Baker's external network. It would be best to get her involved in something outside the home that will still relate to her maternal role and to find her someone other than Mr. Baker to call in an emergency. We will have to work out details during the session. I am tentatively considering a task of her calling her minister to see if the church has any group activities that would involve, either by group definition or by coincidence, other mothers of adolescents. Since this task would put her in contact with the minister, he might ask her what the problem is and thus become a source of support himself. Some of this work could be done in the first session, which would be a good time in terms of the ongoing crisis contributing to motivation. However, the session time is limited, and I wouldn't want to overburden or distract Mrs. Baker by assigning her too many tasks.

If it turns out that Mr. Baker will attend the second session, then I'll probably want Bill also; otherwise, I probably won't. Depending on how it goes, I might just leave it up to him ("Why don't you think about our meeting next week.

There might be some things you'd like to bring up, or sometimes kids just like to hear what's going on, anyway. You can see what you think about coming.").

Whoever comes, some limited rehashing of the work of the first session might be needed, and the tasks will certainly need to be followed up. Some further intervention or referral for Bill might be indicated.

If the first session has proceeded as planned, and particularly if Mr. and Mrs. Baker follow through on their tasks, the crisis will probably be almost over before the second session. Thus the issue of closing must be considered even before the second session. Of course, any of a number of obstacles could arise. Otherwise, following the first session I anticipate one phone call and then one more session—maybe only with Mrs. Baker—and then two more phone calls. Some more useful work *may* be done—assisting the parents in dealing with the school, some specific moves concerning Bill, or encouraging Mrs. Baker to get a job or some other interest. We may even deal directly with the issue of the last child, since I mentioned it already and no one got upset, but that is beginning to move toward therapy and a few more sessions.

In contrast to these plans, when I call, the family may say they have decided that they don't even need a second session. Or, they may not show up, in which case I'll call them and ask how they're doing. There are various possibilities— they may be in another crisis and have turned elsewhere for help; they may feel everything's resolved now, either after the session or by their having done something totally different from anything we discussed; or they might have "just forgot." In any event, my task will be to commend them for settling their crisis so well and for their resourcefulness. I will mention that for many families adolescence seems to involve one problem after another. I'll tell them that they should feel free to call me again sometime, maybe just to talk about what's happening. At the same time I will carefully turn away any credit in the unlikely event that it is given. I'll ask if I may call again in a couple of months to see how things have worked out.

This, then, is a tentative assessment and plan for the first session and for the whole intervention. The plan partially evolved from whatever data were available prior to the first session, but it evolved mainly during the early part of the first session. The plan is subject to continuing modification as the session and the intervention unfolds. It is essential to formulate such an assessment and plan as early as possible, as well as to be flexible about it thereafter. Clearly this formulation is not "correct" but only one of many possible formulations. The goal is not to find the "correct" formulation but to arrive at one that will work. In general, the more correct the formulation, the more likely it is to work.

In practice, the case on which this presentation is based did not go quite this way. The father continued to come but remained rather uninvolved. I made an early error of trying to get him more involved. The crisis was resolved—rather easily, in fact. The family then drifted into family therapy, largely due to Mrs. Baker's unrealistic attachment to me and the son's continuing depression, and somewhat in spite of the father's passive reluctance. Eventually there was another crisis, some therapy with the son, and the case ended—a modest success if the goals were modest, a moderate failure if the goals were for deep and significant change in the family dynamics. The crisis intervention portion described here was a success in terms of its own goals. It appeared that seeds planted during the crisis intervention led eventually to more closeness and support between the son and the father, to slightly diminished entanglement between the son and the mother, and to the son later making some use of individual therapy, that is, using the therapist as an addition to his network.

Appendix

A Crisis Intervention Course

This book evolved from a course in crisis intervention that has been well received by a wide range of mental health professionals and paraprofessionals, but especially by workers in the Baltimore County (Md.) Department of Juvenile Services and the Baltimore and Carroll County Departments of Social Services. These workers found that their previous training and experience had left them poorly equipped to deal with the occasional crisis situations that arose in the course of their routine work. These crises seemed to require inordinate amounts of time and effort, while frequently ending in frustration and grief. These workers particularly appreciated getting an organized approach that they could follow and specific techniques that they could apply. The course was organized and presented to maximize its relevancy to their daily work. Hopefully this book may be used as a text or source book for similar courses given by mental health professionals to similar groups.

The book is organized much like the material presented in the course, generally following the sequence of an actual crisis intervention. Each session consisted of a lecture and a discussion, usually with a role-playing exercise or demonstration. There were written homework exercises and assigned readings. The course was usually presented in seven sessions of eighty minutes each.

Course Outline

Session 1.

Lecture: introduction
crisis theory
Principles 1–6

Homework: describe a typical crisis that occurs in your job and discuss in terms of the definition of crisis

Reading: G. Caplan, *Principles of Preventive Psychiatry.* New York: Basic Books, 1964, pp. 38–49. T. Gordon. *P.E.T.: Parent Effectiveness Training.* New York: Peter H. Wyden, 1970, chapter on active listening.

Session 2.

Lecture: Principles 7–10
Step 1

Exercise: active listening demonstrated and then practiced in pairs

Homework: practice active listening
analyze sample case using Aquilera and Messick's model

Reading: Caplan, appendix B, pp. 288–296

Session 3.

Lecture: Steps 1–3
role playing

Exercise: demonstration of role playing

Reading: N. Golan, "Short-Term Crisis Intervention." *Child Welfare,* 1971, *1* (2).

Session 4.
    Lecture: Step 4
                   clear communication
                   plussing, paradox, tasks
    Exercise: demonstration of beginning a case
    Homework: sample case—analyze and plan
Session 5.
    Lecture: Step 5
                   anticipatory planning, network
                   bargaining
    Exercise: sample case—group analysis and planning
    Homework: define your job role in terms of your ca-
                   pacities and your limitations
    Reading: E. Berne, *Games People Play.* New York:
                   Grove Press, 1964, pp. 117–119, 143–147.
Session 6.
    Lecture: obstacles
    Exercise: demonstration of bargaining
    Homework: discuss an experience using something
                   from this course in your work, and reasons
                   for success or failure
    Reading: La Vietes, "Crisis Intervention for Ghetto
                   Children." *American Journal of Orthopsychi-
                   atry,* 1974, *44* (5), 720–727.
Session 7.
    Lecture: Steps 6–7
                   special issues
    Exercise: discussion, review, and evaluation of entire
                   course

Index

221